EDVARD MUNCH

THE SOLOMON R. GUGGENHEIM MUSEUM, NEW YORK

EDVARD MUNCH, in the United States, is more admired than known. Only a very few of his important works have found their way into public or private collections in this country. In New York museums, for example, his paintings are virtually unrepresented despite his acknowledged position as a pivotal innovator of the modern era.

It has not been easy to borrow for this exhibition from the more fortunate Scandinavian, German, and Swiss sources. Owners, aware of the rare values in their possession are understandably reluctant to part with these, even for a brief period of time. As a result, the only Munch exhibition organized by an American museum prior to the current effort, goes back to 1950 when the Institute of Contemporary Art introduced the Norwegian master's work in Boston, sharing it subsequently with ten other cities including New York. The time seemed ripe, therefore, to acquaint a new and to re-acquaint older generations with the contribution of this great modern pioneer. Long standing plans of The Solomon R. Guggenheim Museum assumed tangible form when at the opening of Oslo's Munch Museum in 1963, Director Johan H. Langaard undertook to lend the weight of his influence to the organization of a full-scale retrospective showing at the Guggenheim Museum. Ready agreement to participate in such an exhibition and to aid it most generously was subsequently obtained from Dr. Sigurd Willoch, Director of Norway's National Gallery and from Jan Askeland, Director of the Rasmus Meyer Collection in Bergen. Private collectors in Norway and, eventually, museums and collectors throughout the world followed suit. Separately listed in this catalogue, they are entitled to every gratitude which, as organizers, we are privileged to extend.

The selection of the works and the preparation of this catalogue proceeded in close consultation and with every support of Norwegian Museum officials. Among these, extensive and essential contributions have been made by Reidar Revold, and Leif Østby, respectively Curators of the Munch Museum and of the National Gallery in Oslo. By providing a major share of the printed documentation these distinguished scholars have placed at our disposal the results of years of diligent research. Lastly, I wish to acknowledge the very far-reaching assistance rendered through all phases of the preparatory process by Dr. Louise Averill Svendsen, the Guggenheim's Associate Curator, who also added her selection of Munch's works on paper to my choice of paintings.

Thomas M. Messer   Director, The Solomon R. Guggenheim Museum

LENDERS TO THE EXHIBITION

Johan Henrik Andresen, Oslo

Nicolai A. Andresen, Oslo

Mr. and Mrs. Nils Astrup, Oslo

Mr. and Mrs. Sigval Bergesen, d.y., Oslo

Jørgen W. Cappelen, Oslo

Thorvald Johnsen, Oslo

A. Fredrik Klaveness, Oslo

Haakon Thomas Onstad, Munkedal, Sweden

Bergen Billedgalleri, Bergen

Rasmus Meyers Samlinger, Bergen

Museum of Fine Arts, Boston

The Detroit Institute of Arts

Städt. Galerie im Landesmuseum, Hannover

Ateneumin Taidemuseo, Helsinki

Munch-museet, Oslo

Nasjonalgalleriet, Oslo

Museum of Art, Carnegie Institute, Pittsburgh

Národní Galerie, Prague

Nationalmuseum, Stockholm

Staatsgalerie, Stuttgart

Kunsthaus, Zürich

CHRONOLOGY

This account of the artist's life is based on the information published in *Edvard Munch fra År til År. A Year by Year Record of Edvard Munch's Life,* by Johan H. Langaard and Reidar Revold, Oslo, H. Aschehoug & Co., 1961.

1863   Born December 12 at Engelhaugen Farm in Løten, Hedmark County, Norway, son of Army Medical Corps doctor Christian Munch and his wife Laura Cathrine Bjølstad.

1864   His parents moved to Oslo, then called Christiania.

1868   His mother died of tuberculosis; his aunt Miss Karen Bjølstad took over the household.

1877   His sister Sophie died of tuberculosis at the age of 15.

1879   Entered Technical College to train as an engineer.

1880   Began seriously to paint. November, left Technical College.

1881   Entered Royal School of Design, attending first freehand and later modeling class, under the sculptor Julius Middelthun.

1882   Rented a studio with six fellow artists; their work supervised by the painter Christian Krohg.

1883   June, included in first group exhibition, Oslo. Autumn, attended Frits Thaulow's "open-air academy" at Modum.

1884   Came in contact with the Bohemian set, the avant-garde of contemporary naturalistic painters and writers in Norway. Received first of several grants for continued studies.

1885   In May, on a scholarship from the painter Frits Thaulow, traveled via Antwerp to Paris where he stayed for three weeks. Visited the Salon and the Louvre; particularly impressed by Manet. After the summer at Borre returned to Oslo to begin three of his major works: *The Sick Child, The Morning After, Puberty.*

1886   Completed *The Sick Child,* the first of several versions.

1889   April, first one-man exhibition, Oslo. Received State scholarship of 1500 kroner for study abroad. To Paris in October where he entered Léon Bonnat's art school. November his father died. Moved to St. Cloud in December.

1890   Continued to attend Bonnat's art school; moved primarily in Norwegian circle of artists, poets and writers. Summer in Norway. On renewal of State scholarship sailed for France, but was hospitalized with rheumatic fever for two months in Le Havre.

1891	January-April in Nice to recover health; May in Paris; Norway in the summer. After third renewal of State scholarship returned to Paris; in December to Nice.
1892	Left Nice at end of March for Norway to arrange large one-man exhibition at Oslo in September. Invited by *Verein Berliner Künstler* to exhibit in Berlin, where his paintings stirred such violent protest that the show was closed after one week. The German artists who supported Munch, led by Max Liebermann, subsequently withdrew from the society to found their own association, the *Berlin Secession*. The exhibition shown thereafter at Düsseldorf, Cologne and Berlin.
1893	Munch spent the greater part of his time in Germany until 1908, with stays in Paris and summers in Norway. Exhibited extensively in Germany, Paris and Scandinavia. Moved in circle of literary men and critics including August Strindberg, Richard Dehmel, Julius Meier-Graefe and the Polish poet Stanislaw Przybyszewski. Worked on *Frieze of Life* series, completing *Madonna, The Cry, Vampire, Death and the Maiden*.
1894	Produced his first etchings. First monograph on his work by Przybyszewski, Meier-Graefe, Servaes and Pastor. First lithographs.
1895	June, visit to Paris; Meier-Graefe published portfolio of etchings. *La Revue Blanche* reproduced the lithograph *The Cry*.
1896	To Paris in February; first woodcuts and color lithographs. Worked on illustrations for Baudelaire's *Les Fleurs du Mal*. April-May, 10 paintings shown in *Salon des Indépendants*. June exhibition at Bing's gallery, L'Art Nouveau, reviewed by Strindberg in *La Revue Blanche*.
1897	10 paintings shown in *Salon des Indépendants*. Summer in Åsgårdstrand.
1898	Partly in Norway and Germany.
1899	Spring, trip to Italy. Autumn and winter convalescing in Norwegian sanitarium.
1900	March to Berlin, Florence and Rome; sanitarium in Switzerland. Autumn and winter in Norway. Completed *Dance of Life*.
1901	Partly in Norway and Germany.
1902	Winter and spring in Berlin. Introduced to Dr. Max Linde who became his patron, purchasing *Fertility* and commissioning a portfolio of 16 prints. At the end of an unfortunate love affair, he lost one joint of a finger on his left hand from a gunshot wound. In December, met Gustav Schiefler who bought several graphic works and started systematic cataloguing of Munch's prints. Exhibited 22 works from *Frieze of Life* series at *Berlin Secession*.
1903	Trip to Paris where exhibited in *Salon des Indépendants*. Three visits to Lübeck; worked on portraits of Dr. Linde and his four young sons.
1904	Concluded important contract with dealers Bruno Cassirer, Berlin, and Commeter, Hamburg, for sole rights to sale of Munch prints and paintings in Germany. Became regular member of *Berlin Secession*, which Beckmann, Nolde and Kandinsky joined a year later.
1905	Involved in violent quarrel with artist Ludvig Karsten. This incident is believed to have inspired two 1935 works, *The Fight* and *The Uninvited Guest*. Important exhibition at "Mánes," Prague.
1906	Drafted designs for two Ibsen plays, in Berlin, *Ghosts* and *Hedda Gabler*. Painted portrait of Friedrich Nietzsche at request of Swedish banker Ernest Thiel who subsequently commissioned and purchased a great many of his oils.
1908	Started series of pictures based on workmen and industry. Jens Thiis, Director of Nasjonalgalleriet, Oslo, purchased several works for the museum over strong opposition. Despite evident success, entered clinic of Dr. Daniel Jacobson in Copenhagen as result of nervous breakdown.

1909   Spent winter and spring at the clinic. Composed and illustrated prose poem *Alpha and Omega*. Entered design competition for decoration of Oslo University Fest:val Hall (*Aula murals*). The Norwegian collector Rasmus Meyer purchased several of his works. Major show in Oslo, at Blomqvist's, of 100 oils and 200 graphics.

1910   Winter and spring at Kragerø. Bought Ramme estate at Hvitsten on the Oslo Fjord to increase working facilities.

1911   Won Oslo University competition.

1912   Included in show of contemporary Scandinavian art sponsored by the *American Scandinavian Society*, New York, believed to be the first American showing of his works. Among 6 oils were versions of *Sick Child, Starlight Night* and *In the Orchard (Adam and Eve under the Apple Tree)*. Received generally favorable reviews. Honorary guest of the *Sonderbund*, Cologne.

1913   Represented in the Armory Show, New York, by 8 graphics. Shown were versions of *Vampire, Moonlight, The Lonely Ones, Madonna* and *Nude with Red Hair*. Lent by the artist, Munch priced them at $200 each. Received numerous tributes on occasion of 50th birthday.

1914   May 29, Oslo University accepted *Aula* murals.

1915   At his third American show, in the *Panama-Pacific International Exposition*, San Francisco, awarded gold medal for his graphics. 10 oils were also exhibited. Now successful enough to give financial aid to young German artists.

1916   Bought house, Ekely, at Skøyen outside Oslo where he spent most of his time when not traveling. The Oslo University murals were unveiled, with resulting rise in his reputation.

1917   Curt Glaser's book on Munch published.

1918   Wrote brochure, *The Frieze of Life*, for an exhibition of the frieze paintings at Blomqvist's in Oslo. Continued working with the *Aula* and *Frieze of Life* motifs.

1919-1921   Continued frequent travels.

1922   Painted 12 murals for the workers' dining room in the Freia Chocolate Factory, Oslo. Major retrospective of 73 oils and 389 graphics held at Kunsthaus, Zürich.

1923-1927   Continued support of German artists. Frequent trips throughout Scandinavia and Germany. Many exhibitions.

1927   His most comprehensive show held at the Nationalgalerie, Berlin, included 223 oils. Later, show enlarged at Nasjonalgalleriet, Oslo.

1928   Worked on designs for murals for the central hall of Oslo City Hall.

1929   Built "winter studio" at Ekely. Major graphics show in the Nationalmuseum, Stockholm.

1933   70th birthday brought numerous tributes. Monographs by Jens Thiis and Pola Gauguin published. New designs for the *Alma Mater* in the *Aula*.

1937   82 works by Munch in German museums branded "degenerate" and confiscated. These were later sold in Norway.

1940-1944   Lived quietly during German occupation of Norway. Refused any contact with Nazi invaders and Quislings. Continued to paint and work with prints.

1944   January 23, a little more than a month after his 80th birthday, he died peacefully at Ekely. To the Municipality of Oslo he bequeathed all the work he left behind: approximately 1,000 paintings 15,000 prints, 4,400 watercolors and drawings, and 6 sculptures—now in the Munch-museet, Oslo, opened 1963.

THE EARLY MUNCH

BY SIGURD WILLOCH

Edvard Munch was 17 years old in 1880 when he decided to become an artist. From then until his death in 1944 at the age of 80, he worked ceaselessly, producing an enormous body of paintings, drawings, watercolors and graphics; an *oeuvre* ranging from small, intimate paintings and etchings to monumental wall decorations.

The young Munch was impressionable and open to many influences. Though he studied only very briefly with the sculptor Julius Middelthun at the School of Design in Oslo, Middelthun's classical style may have influenced Munch's feeling for form in drawing. He lived in Oslo among a lively and argumentative group of French-inspired painters, and his sensibility was shaped by them and marked by the social conflicts dominating the era. The naturalist painter Christian Krohg influenced him when he supervised his work in 1882. A still bolder naturalism emerged in his painting after he had studied at Frits Thaulow's open-air academy in 1883. Munch's earliest work is characterized by its intimacy of subject, delicate form and charming color. His motifs are drawn from the family and its milieu, the town in which he lived and the surrounding countryside. An elevated sense of color is already apparent in these canvases of the early 1880's.

Munch visited Paris for the first time in the spring of 1885, and was overwhelmed by the modern painting he saw there. Manet in particular impressed him deeply, and the Impressionists appealed strongly to him, their technique soon filtering into his own work.

Munch spent the summers in small towns like Åsgårdstrand on the Oslo Fjord, often in the company of friends. There he absorbed the feeling of the bright Nordic summer night, which he interpreted in his most popular paintings of great spreading trees on the mysteriously illuminated shoreline. Typical of these paintings is *Summer Night:* the artist's sister Inger is shown sitting on a stone near the water, figure and nature melting together. The naturalistic strain is particularly apparent in Munch's canvases of the late 80's, for example the large *Spring* and *Military Band on Karl Johan Street,* of 1889.

But Munch could not confine himself within the limits of naturalism. He needed a richer, freer and more individual form language with which to express the ideas that occupied him—memories of illness in his family, his sister's death, and his friends' preoccupation with sex which at once attracted and repelled him. After his study-tour of 1885-86 Munch painted his youthful masterpiece *The Sick Child,* a theme to which he was to return again and again in the course of the next 40 years. In this first remarkable version, Munch expresses his love for his family, releasing painful memories of childhood experience. The composition is based on a simple scheme which concentrates attention on the meeting of the two heads—the invalid's pale profile and the mother's dark, bowed head.

The powerful composition and the use of color to express spiritual and emotional content far surpass ordinary naturalism. The work is a confession: its deeply personal content is like a spirit that Munch must exorcise over and over again. Munch's art and its development can be explained only in relation to his life. He expressed this himself when he said "My art has given my life a meaning, I was seeking the light through it. It has been a stick to lean on which I needed."

The Sick Child was not an isolated phenomenon in Munch's work of this period. Though still working in a technique that may be called Impressionist and naturalistic, by the mid-80's Munch was already very much concerned with ideas we associate with the Symbolist movement of the 1890's, and which he embodied in the *Frieze of Life* series. He painted the first versions of ideas for this series, *The Day After* and *Puberty*, in 1886. Unfortunately, both of these canvases have been destroyed.

Munch went to Paris again in 1889 and worked in the studio of Léon Bonnat, a fashionable naturalist. Though he was already an independent artist, he was still open to many influences which were to be of great importance to his later development. He was particularly impressed by Gauguin's simplified figure drawings and compositional ideas, and Degas' unique and startling compositional devices. A number of tendencies are reflected in Munch's work of this period: the canvases of St. Cloud and Nice with their prevailing blue tones and lyrical atmosphere, and the bright, gay street scenes of Paris and Oslo, executed in a fully developed Impressionist technique.

The early 1890's were the beginning of an era of feverish activity, conflict and fame for Munch. He developed a radical new form-language for his deeply personal feelings and ideas. His art may now truly be called expressionist. 1892 was a particularly significant year: Munch exhibited his new paintings in Oslo and was invited to participate in the Verein Berliner Künstler. The latter exhibition aroused scandalized protest and was closed after a week. When the paintings of the Verein Berliner Künstler were shown later in Düsseldorf, Cologne and elsewhere in Berlin, the ensuing publicity made Munch famous as a radical of contemporary art.

Munch lived for the most part in Germany until 1908, and associated with a circle of writers which included August Strindberg, Gunnar Heiberg, the Norwegian dramatist, and the Polish poet Stanislaw Przybyszewski. It was during this period that Munch worked intensively on the series *The Frieze of Life*. He envisioned the series as a modern conception of love and death, indeed a philosophical interpretation of the whole of life. Current ideas of women as demonic, fate-destined powers are central to Munch's concept of the series.

Munch expresses his ideas through symbolic color, Art Nouveau inspired line, and, above all, in his powerful draftsmanship. This expressive drawing is especially notable in such paintings as *Puberty, Death in the Sick Chamber, Madonna, Woman in Three Phases* and *Ashes*. The *Frieze of Life* is not an entirely consistent whole, either in technique or concept, for Munch developed and changed as he worked on its separate components. He could not possibly sustain the same youthful feelings about life in the later works that he had expressed in the early paintings, and many new ideas emerged by the turn of the century. Compare, for example, a milestone in the artist's work, *The Dance of Life*, a complex summation of Munch's feelings about eroticism, touched with bitter scorn, with the earlier, simpler *Woman in Three Phases*.

In 1894 Munch made his first etchings and lithographs. His visit to Paris in 1895 was of major significance to the development of his graphic work. Gauguin, Toulouse-Lautrec, the graphics of Redon, the Symbolists and the Synthesists, in fact the whole milieu of the Paris art world stimulated his interest and inspired him to renew his study of reality. Meier-Graefe published a portfolio of his etchings, and Thadée Natanson, the editor of *La Revue Blanche*, became interested in his graphics. 1896 was a decisive year: Munch exhibited at the Salon des Indépendants and at Bing's *L'Art Nouveau*; he met Stephane Mallarmé and executed the poet's portrait in lithograph and etching, and he began his illustrations for Baudelaire's *Les Fleurs du Mal*.

Munch had first turned to graphics as a change from painting. Soon, however, etchings, lithographs and woodcuts became as important to him as his painting. He discovered that the graphic medium offered him a new outlet with new possibilities for the expression of the same ideas and feelings he was concerned with in painting. He found that woodcuts were particularly suited to his talents and produced some of his finest prints in this technique. An instinctive master of graphics, Munch's great prints—for example *The Girl and Death, The Girls and the Skeleton, The Kiss, Madonna,* and *The Sick Child*—help to place him in the very front rank of European artists.

Munch's early work is often contrasted with his production after 1909. He is seen as the gloomy, pensive 19th-century artist who was abruptly reborn as the life-asserting creator of the Aula murals. Certainly, Munch's work is varied and embraces extreme polarities of feeling and expression. But his development is coherent, consistent and unbroken, as an examination of his work of the first decade of the 20th century reveals.

Though these were turbulent years for Munch—years marked by controversies with old friends, a restless and irregular mode of life, constant traveling, and eventually, in 1908, a nervous breakdown necessitating a stay in Dr. Daniel Jacobson's nerve clinic near Copenhagen—the amount of work he produced during this period is overwhelming. This *oeuvre* consists of graphics and oils, figure compositions and landscapes. There are new versions of motifs treated in previous years; and new ideas and techniques emerged, yet the thread connecting these new works with Munch's past and future production is always evident.

A major interest of Munch during the first years of the century were life-size, front-face portraits, usually of men. Although the many portraits he painted in this format plainly have their roots in his earlier painting, they clearly forecast the monumental aspect of his later work. The concept of masculine vitality and strength embodied in these canvases far surpasses the characterizations of the 90's.

Just as in his earlier work, Munch in this period expressed extremes of both despair and lyricism. Thus, on the one hand, there is the series of landscapes in shining color from Åsgårdstrand, so much like his earlier landscapes, the soft, lyrical summer night of *Girls on the Bridge* and the chill winter night of the Oslo Fjord in *White Night.* The despairing and disillusioned Munch of the 1890's revealed his bitterness again in the *Self-Portrait* of 1906 and the violent, erotic fantasy *Marat's Death.* But there is much that is new in these canvases. For Munch developed a vigorous and free painting technique at this time. A forceful Fauvism, this method of using broad strips of strongly contrasted color stresses the violent character of his subjects. This fresh new manner of painting marks the series of landscapes painted in Lübeck and Warnemünde in 1907-08, of which *Bathing Men* is a major example. In its clarity of concept and sober form, *Bathing Men* points forward to the monumental Aula decorations. It must be stressed, however, that the monumentality emergent in this work and in the large portraits was always latent in Munch's paintings. *Fertility,* a composition of ornamental clarity, and the portrait of Inger and *Mother and Daughter* are a few examples of works of the 90's that reveal this implicit monumentality.

When Munch returned to Norway in 1909 after many years of travel and living abroad, he was 45 years old. His youth was past and his achievement was already enormous. He had created an impressive, masterful body of work and had become famous abroad, often under extremely difficult conditions. The recognition he had won abroad he now began to achieve in his native land. He no longer felt homeless. Artistically, his homecoming meant not a break, but a continuity. He now stood at the threshold of a new era in his life—the threshold of wider artistic development throughout the years.

THE LATE MUNCH

BY JOHAN H. LANGAARD

Edvard Munch, even more than most modern painters, waged a long and bitter struggle before achieving recognition. All indications point to the successful completion of this achievement: The Solomon R. Guggenheim Museum is organizing a major and lavish exhibition of his work, an enterprise involving the dispatch of his major work from Europe to America. Publications on his art are constantly increasing and are being printed in many languages. His paintings and prints have registered record prices. During the last 10 or 15 years, forgeries of his works have made their appearance on the international art market, a curious sort of compliment.

The name of Edvard Munch has attained the same international acclaim and reputation as that of his countrymen Henrik Ibsen and Edvard Grieg. Of the three, however, the least is known today about Munch. One reason for this may be that his later production is apt to be eclipsed by his work of the 1890's—the early period upon which Munch's international recognition is founded. But it would be regrettable if the accomplishments of the early period should blind art lovers to the fact that after 1900, and, indeed, until the day of his death, Munch underwent an unbroken development as an artist, moving towards a liberation of his form language which reached its climax in 1916, with the completion of the University murals.

This process was already under way when Munch arrived in Copenhagen from Warnemünde in 1908, to hold an exhibition. At this time he suffered a nervous collapse and found it necessary to commit himself for medical treatment and took a rest cure in Dr. Daniel Jacobson's nerve clinic. Shortly after his arrival in this institution he was hard at work at his painting as well as his print-making. He wrote and illustrated in a new series of lithographs his strange prose poem *Alpha and Omega*, in which he ridiculed love and sex relationships. It was there also that he produced one of his loveliest drypoint etchings, the portrait of the young nurse Linke Jørgensen.

When Munch was admitted to the clinic there was probably no one of whom he stood in greater awe than his doctor, who had the power to declare him mentally deranged, and to commit him for the rest of his life. He therefore concentrated on the object of his fear, and painted a full-length, front-face portrait showing the authoritative doctor in a posture of unshakable self-confidence and superior knowledge, qualities that were obviously exaggerated by the dependent patient undergoing a nervous crisis. In reality, the worthy professor was comical rather than awesome—his air of pompous vanity was mitigated by his friendliness. The model's personality is conveyed with an expressionist intensity of color far surpassing anything Munch had so far achieved, and the figure and the surrounding space merge more effectively than ever before in his portraiture.

The interlude in the Jacobson nerve clinic, which lasted over half a year, marks no break in the artist's activity, nor did it lead to a stagnation of his development. Nevertheless, the year 1908-1909 proved to be a turning point in his life. In the clinic he made a number of resolutions. He foreswore sleeping draughts and excessive use of stimulants, and abandoned the unsettled, restless life away from his native country that he had pursued for the preceding twenty years. He decided to find a quiet spot in Norway where he could pursue his artistic aims undisturbed. Isolation was imperative if he was to devote himself to the execution of the *Frieze of Life* as a mural, the form in which he had originally planned the work.

In the summer of 1909 he returned to Norway, and shortly thereafter took a lease on a property in Kragerø, a small town on the coast of the outer Oslo Fjord. It was a safe distance from the capital, where he had met so much opposition and where he would always risk meeting many of his more or less imaginary enemies. Occasionally, when an old friend, such as Thorvald Stang, looked him up in his retreat at Kragerø, he would paint his picture, adding to his impressive series of large-scale portraits. Munch referred to these life-size portraits as his artistic bodyguard. These portraits belong to a sequence that can be traced back to the Manet-influenced pictures of Jensen-Hjell and *The Ship Owner* of 1885 and 1889. The series includes his portraits of Consul Sandberg and Professor Jacobson of 1901 and 1908, and continues until 1932, with pictures of a Norwegian society lady and a Swiss professor. Munch once said of his portraiture, "I must aim at the target, and if I do hit it, I score a bull's eye." The remark is apt: as presentations of human character his portraits are no less searching and revealing than the *Frieze of Life* in its vision of modern man's psyche.

Inspired by the primeval looking rock formations and the clear light of the coastal scenery, Munch created, during the years after 1909, a series of landscapes. Like *Winter, Kragerø* of 1912, these are, as a rule, characterized by a new-found sense of calm and simplicity in their composition, which is further enhanced by the cool tones of Munch's palette. In many of these landscapes Munch depicts the working man and the rhythm of his toil set against the panorama of the seasons. He saw the working man as marked by his struggle for existence: strong, upright and weatherbeaten as the fir tree he fells, the lumberjack wields his axe in the forest. The masterpiece of this genre is the dynamically composed *Workers on Their Way Home* of 1915. Though the color reveals Impressionist features, it is primarily employed for expressive ends. Indeed, it is principally by means of this powerfully expressive use of color that Munch conveys in the canvas the feeling of solidarity behind the 20th century's triumphant labor movement.

Once he had settled at Kragerø, Munch began sketches for a competition for a mural commission for the Oslo University festival hall. The murals were to be commissioned in connection with the University's impending centenary celebrations of 1911. In Oslo, especially in academic quarters, Munch's sketches for the murals were regarded with a mixture of suspicion and incomprehension. But this attitude did not shake Munch's resolve to win the competition, and the commission was finally awarded to him. Work on a decorative project of this kind must have made Munch as happy as a man of his temperament could possibly be. He was more prolific while working on the murals than he had ever been. Deciding that his quarters were too cramped, he looked for new homes and moved, in 1910 and again in 1913, to larger houses on the coast, nearer to the capital.

At first, Munch thought that the *Frieze of Life*, which had long occupied his attention, would be a suitable theme for the University murals. He soon realized, however, that the erotic and morbid nature of the motifs he had chosen might be offensive and out of place at the University. These considerations and the architectural demands of the festival hall induced him to use a different cycle of motifs in the sketches he submitted.

In the completed murals the sun, representing the light-giving qualities of knowledge and research, occupies the focal position. From the white heat of its orb, life-giving rays reach out to warm our world, dispelling the darkness of the winter night and rousing man from his slumbers.

Everything the sunlight reveals in nature excites the curiosity and exploratory urge of man, who reaches out to gather the fruits of knowledge and quenches his thirst in its inexhaustible well. In the light of the sun, life on earth runs its course and history is the record of this eternal process. The paintings are based on the landscapes of the outer Oslo Fjord and depict natural and common-place incidents of everyday life. Painted in a surprisingly free style with dazzling pure, bright color, and monumental in composition, the murals are universal symbols of the great, eternal forces in life and nature. The narrative cycle is executed in 11 large panels, the largest of which measures a little over 36 feet wide. All are slightly more than 15 feet high.

Munch constantly struggled for recognition, never neglecting an opportunity to exhibit his work in any country where he could do so. In 1912 he was invited to exhibit as guest artist at the Sonderbund in Cologne, and in 1913 at the Armory Show in the United States. By the time his murals were finally installed in the Oslo University festival hall in 1916, he had disarmed the majority of his critics both at home and abroad. After the first large retrospective exhibition of his work, arranged by W. Wartmann at the Zürich Kunsthaus in 1922, Munch's fame and popularity grew rapidly. His most successful exhibition, however, was undoubtedly the one-man show presented in 1927 at the national galleries of Oslo and Berlin by their respective directors Jens Thiis and Dr. Justi.

Success did not make Munch slacken his pace, though he was now, admittedly, more relaxed about many aspects of his life, turning his gaze more and more often outward to the world about him. Sometimes harrowing and bitter memories did revive, occasioned, for instance, by the news of the death of a cherished friend. This usually provoked a nervous crisis which he was compelled to analyze in the mirror of his art, and he produced a steadily growing number of self-portraits. At intervals printmaking absorbed him, providing a challenge to his creative imagination. In 1915-1917 he made a large number of fresh impressions of various old woodcuts, experimenting with up to 18 color variations. At the same time, the countryside around him, the wealth of color in the air itself and the freedom of space, filled him with a spontaneous and overwhelming desire to paint, resulting in a great number of large and harmonious landscapes, such as *The Man in the Cabbage Field*, of 1916. He continued to work on two large compositions, which he had not completed to his satisfaction when he was painting the University murals. These were the *Human Mountain* and *Alma Mater*. To leave them uncompleted was for Munch as unthinkable as abandoning his plan of creating the *Frieze of Life*.

Munch realized that the completion of the *Frieze of Life*, as well as the many other compositions that he was anxious to begin, would require more spacious quarters than he occupied. He resolved to live in virtual seclusion. In 1916 he bought Ekely, a large property at Skøyen on the outskirts of Oslo, where he lived most of the time, when not traveling, for the rest of his life. The house, which had a farm attached to it, was barred to all but a small circle of friends and the artist's models. For company he had, apart from these chosen few, his dogs, and a horse whose main purpose in life was to serve as a model. The garden was allowed to grow wild, but the house, stable, cowshed and barn were converted into studios and connected with covered walks which also served as open-air studios. The printmaking presses were set up in the cellar of the main house, and after a while the floor was ankle-deep in experimental prints. In 1929 he built a large fireproof winter studio. And yet, as a rule, most of what he produced was left standing where it had been painted, in farm buildings where the fire risk was considerable, in the open-air studios, or simply out in the garden, where pictures might be exposed for years on end to the wind and weather. Munch referred to this treatment as a "horse-doctor's cure", which the canvases were forced to undergo, to ensure the melting colors and the dry, brittle textural effect he wanted. He had neither the time nor the energy—so intensely occupied was he with his work—to bother to look after his completed canvases, to store them in a dry spot, or varnish them.

In 1918 he exhibited the paintings of the life frieze in Oslo. He described it as one of his most important works "if not the most important". "It should", he continued, "likewise be regarded as a part of the University murals, for which in many ways it has been a forerunner, and without which the murals might possibly never have been completed. It developed my decorative sense...." Yet, he compared the frieze to "a wreck which had had half her rigging washed overboard". He was referring to the fact that between 1906 and 1909 he had lost several of the most important components of this work as the result of three major sales: to the Swedish art patron Ernest Thiel, to the National Gallery in Oslo, and to the Norwegian collector Rasmus Meyer in Bergen. He felt that he must recreate the works he had sold, so that the series would be complete and consistent in style. To keep the series intact, Munch decided he would no longer sell his paintings. Fortunately, he was in a position to do this, since the sale of his prints made him financially independent.

During the 1920's and 1930's he produced a large number of woodcuts and lithographs, and until the very end of his life he painted works of great mastery. Perhaps the most poignant of his late paintings is the eloquent self-portrait *Between the Clock and the Bed*, completed in 1940. Munch revealed in it the same fearless self-examination at the age of nearly eighty that he had shown in his youth. This canvas shows him making his way, tired and lonely, from the sun-drenched room in the background towards the cool blue shadows of the foreground, where his bed, as magnificently decorated as a tomb, awaits him. He pauses for a moment to listen to the ticking of the clock, conscious that the inexorable march of time has brought him to the borderline between the world of the living and the world of the dead. He is an old man reconciling himself, calmly and patiently, to the thought of death; but he is also an artist who is able to paint with an almost paradoxically vigorous and youthful directness.

In 1922 the Freia Chocolate Company commissioned Munch to decorate 12 wall panels in the canteen of their Oslo factory. This was not the opportunity for which he had long been waiting, and for which he had prepared so assiduously; he realized that the *Frieze of Life* was no more an appropriate subject for mural décor in a hall where factory and office workers spent their leisure hours than it had been for the University festival hall. The only part of the frieze he could use was the landscape background—though, of course, he would employ the decorative facility he had developed while working on it. He began work, using well balanced, pure, strong color surfaces to impart a continuous frieze-like feeling to his murals.

All his life Munch waited in vain for the chance to realize his *Frieze of Life* as he had always envisaged it: "a poem of life, love and death". That the opportunity never arose is an artistic tragedy the full scope of which is difficult to gauge. Yet his will to work and his preoccupation with decorative problems remained undiminished. As late as 1936 he made a number of large sketches for a mural intended for the council chamber in the Oslo City Hall, but eventually declined to accept the commission. He felt that his strength was gradually deserting him. He suffered from a distressing eye complaint and was constantly harassed by the problems of day-to-day existence, problems which were, of course, vastly increased after the outbreak of the Second World War. When the Germans occupied Norway, he barred the doors of Ekely to the Nazis who admired his work, even though it had been removed from the museums of Germany as "degenerate art". To humble this proud Norwegian, plans were made to requisition Ekely; but these were abandoned when the Germans discovered how Spartan the home of this celebrity was. When Munch was informed of this reprieve he is said to have remarked: "We can be glad we've never suffered from the craze of collecting furniture".

The war in general—and this situation in particular—distressed Munch far more than this lighthearted remark suggests. On April 18th, 1940, only a few days after the treacherous German attack on his country, he resolved a problem about which he had been brooding for years. He had the necessary legal documents drawn up to bequeath, upon his death, his collection of art to the city of Oslo. On December 13th, 1943, from the terrace at Ekely, he watched the conflagration that raged in the inner harbor after the explosion of a German ammunition store on the wharf. In the chill night air he caught a cold from which he never recovered. On January 23rd, 1944, feeling tired, he lay down to rest on a sofa. Later that afternoon, he was found dead.

When his estate was finally settled, it was found to comprise, in addition to 6 sculptures, about 1,000 paintings, 4,400 drawings and watercolors, as well as 15,000 prints of 719 different kinds of graphic work, of which 198 were etchings, 380 lithographs and 141 woodcuts. This was not only an artistically and financially priceless treasure; it was also a collection of superhuman proportions numerically. It would, therefore, be absurd to claim that it consists of nothing but completely finished work. It is, rather, an incredibly rich but mixed collection, the fruits of a great painter's long and diligent life. No one was more keenly aware of the precise nature of this varied art than Munch himself. He described it as "mainly sketches and designs—for large murals. It would only be really interesting if one could see it in its complete context and compare all the studies and sketches with the more finished work".

This is probably one of the reasons a number of competent critics have expressed the opinion that Munch was even greater as a printmaker than as a painter. It is actually very difficult to evaluate the comparative merits of his work in the two media. One thing is certain: when Munch reached the sublime in his art, as he did in every period of his career, he found the perfect expression for his inmost feelings and thoughts, whether his medium was painting or printmaking. All his production—masterpieces, incomplete sketches and designs—was permeated by the same poignant, impressionable sensitivity, and this sensitivity made Edvard Munch first and last a portrayer of man. He was a painter driven by an all-compelling need to express himself. The work of his later years did not have the same influence on the development of European art that his production in the 1890's had, but the enduring value of his art is not the radical form language, which at one time so shocked his contemporaries; it is his uncompromising, tireless response to his artistic conscience. Indeed, one may state that it is with his later, mature work, such as the lithograph portrait of Professor K. E. Schreiner of 1930, the color woodcut *Birgitte* of 1931, and the painting *Between the Clock and the Bed* of 1940—to mention only a few—that Edvard Munch, both as a painter and printmaker, most fully realized his genius.

PAINTINGS IN THE EXHIBITION

1

CATALOGUE

Entries in this catalogue are chronological. References
to exhibitions under each heading are abbreviated and
may be found in detail in the documentation section
which follows on page 101.

1. PORTRAIT OF THE ARTIST'S SISTER INGER. 1884.
   Oil on canvas, 38¼ x 26⅜" (97 x 67 cm.).
   Signed and dated u. l. "E. Munch 1884".
   Collection Nasjonalgalleriet, Oslo.
   Provenance: Gift of Christian Mustad, Oslo.
   Exhibitions: *Annual State Exhibition*, Olso, 1886, no. 127.
   Nationalgalerie, Berlin, 1927, no. 4.
   Nasjonalgalleriet, Oslo, 1927, no. 12.
   Kunstnernes Hus, Oslo, 1932, no. 197.
   Institute of Contemporary Art, Boston, 1950, no. 3.
   Edvard Munch, Brighton, 1951, no. 3.
   Gemeentemuseum, The Hague, 1951-52, no. 3.
   Petit Palais, Paris, 1952, no. 3.

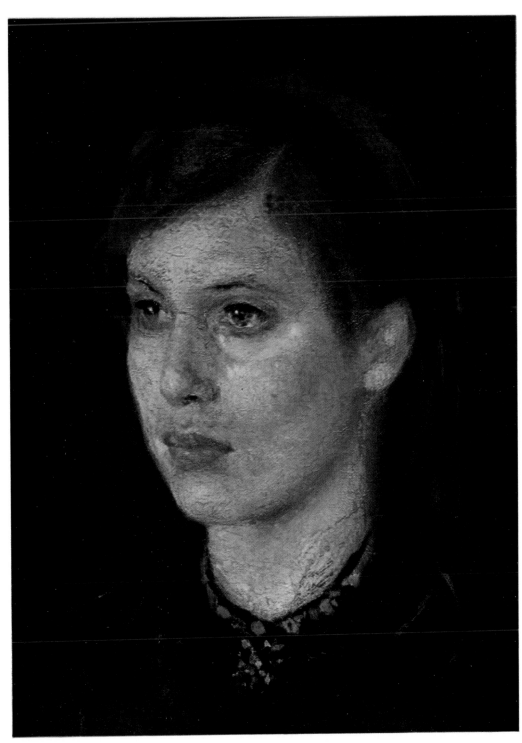

1 (Detail)

2

2. GIRL SITTING ON A BED. 1884.
    Oil on canvas, 37¾ x 40½″ (96,5 x 103,5 cm.).
    Signed and dated l. l. "E. Munch 1884".
    Collection Rasmus Meyers Samlinger, Bergen.
    Provenance: Frits Thaulow, Oslo.
    Exhibitions: *Annual State Exhibition*, Oslo, 1884.
                Architektenhaus, Berlin, 1892, no. 1.
                Georg Kleis, Copenhagen, 1893, no. 1.
                Lichtenberg, Dresden, 1893, no. 1.
                Galerie Blanche, Stockholm, 1894, no. 17.
                Konsthallen, Gothenburg, 1923, no. 197.
                Nasjonalgalleriet, Oslo, 1927, no. 13.
                Gemeentemuseum, The Hague, 1949-50, no. 51.
                Palais des Beaux-Arts, Brussels, 1950, no. 51.
                XXVII Biennale, Venice, 1954, no. 2.
                Haus der Kunst, Munich, 1954, no. 3.
                Kunstforeningen, Copenhagen, 1955, no. 3.

3

3. IN THE DIGS (TÊTE-A-TÊTE). 1885.
Oil on canvas, 25¾ x 29¾″ (65,5 x 75,5 cm.).
Not signed or dated.
Collection Munch-museet, Oslo.
Provenance: Gift of the artist.
Exhibitions: Architektenhaus, Berlin, 1892, no. 25.
Dioramalokalet, Oslo, 1904, no. 3.
Galerie "Mánes", Prague, 1905, no. 63.
Dioramalokalet, Oslo, 1911, no. 80.
Raadhushallen, Copenhagen, 1946, no. 3.
Liljevalchs Konsthall, Stockholm, 1947, no. 3.
Institute of Contemporary Art, Boston, 1950, no. 4.
Edvard Munch, Brighton, 1951, no. 4.
Gemeentemuseum, The Hague, 1951-52, no. 4.
Kunstmuseum, Bern, 1958, no. 1.
Museum Boymans-van Beuningen, Rotterdam, 1958-59, no. 1.
Akademie der Bildenden Künste, Vienna, 1959, no. 1.

4

5

4. PORTRAIT OF THE PAINTER KARL JENSEN-HJELL. 1885.
Oil on canvas, 75 x 39½″ (190 x 100 cm.).
Signed and dated l. l. "E. Munch 1885".
Private Collection, Oslo.
Provenance: Henrik A. Th. Dedichen, Oslo.
Exhibitions: *Annual State Exhibition*, Oslo, 1885.
          Students' Association, Oslo, 1889.
          Jeweler Tostrup's Building, Oslo, 1892, no. 41.
          Architektenhaus, Berlin, 1892, no. 50.
          Georg Kleis, Copenhagen, 1893, no. 49.
          Lichtenberg, Dresden, 1893, no. 49.
          Galerie Blanche, Stockholm, 1894, no. 8.
          Nasjonalgalleriet, Oslo, 1927, no. 18.
          Kunstnernes Hus, Oslo, 1932, no. 198.
          Kunstnernes Hus, Oslo, 1951, no. 31.
          Kunsthaus, Zürich, 1952, no. 1.
          XXVII Biennale, Venice, 1954, no. 1.
          Haus der Kunst, Munich, 1954, no. 5.
          Kunstforeningen, Copenhagen, 1955, no. 5.
          Kunstmuseum, Bern, 1958, no. 2.
          Akademie der Bildenden Künste, Vienna, 1959, no. 2.
          Museum Narodowe, Warsaw, 1959, no. 2.
          Steinernes Haus, Frankfurt am Main, 1962-63, no. 1.
          Nasjonalgalleriet, Oslo, 1964, no. 52.
          Kunsthalle, Kiel, 1964, no. 54.

5. EVENING HOUR WITH THE ARTIST'S SISTER LAURA
(THE YELLOW HAT). 1888.
Oil on canvas, 29½ x 39⅝″ (75 x 100,5 cm.).
Signed and dated l. r. "Edvard Munch 1888".
Collection Thorvald Johnsen, Oslo.
Provenance: J. Sejersted Bødtker, Oslo.
Exhibitions: *Annual State Exhibition*, Oslo, 1888, no. 108.
          Nationalgalerie, Berlin, 1927, no. 16.
          Nasjonalgalleriet, Oslo, 1927, no. 32.
          Kunstnernes Hus, Oslo, 1932, no. 199.
          Institute of Contemporary Art, Boston, 1950, no. 5.
          Gemeentemuseum, The Hague, 1951-52, no. 5.
          Museum Narodowe, Warsaw, 1959, no. 3.
          Steinernes Haus, Frankfurt am Main, 1962-63, no. 4.

6

6. MILITARY BAND ON KARL JOHAN STREET, OSLO. 1889.
Oil on canvas, 40⅛ x 55¾″ (102 x 141,5 cm.).
Signed and dated l. l. "E. Munch 1889".
Collection Kunsthaus, Zürich.
Provenance: Mr. With, Oslo.
              Oskar Moll, Vienna.
              Dr. Curt Glaser, Berlin.
              Nationalgalerie, Berlin.
Exhibitions: *Annual State Exhibition*, Oslo, 1890, no. 92.
              Galerie Alfred Flechtheim, Düsseldorf, 1914, no. 3.
              Nationalgalerie, Berlin, 1927, no. 20.
              Nasjonalgalleriet, Oslo, 1927, no. 36.
              Stedelijk Museum, Amsterdam, 1937, no. 8.
              Ausstellung Edvard Munch 1863-1944, Cologne, Hamburg, Lübeck, 1951, no. 1.
              Kunsthaus, Zürich, 1952, no. 4.
              XXVII Biennale, Venice, 1954, no. 18.
              Haus der Kunst, Munich, 1954, no. 12.
              Kunstmuseum, Bern, 1958, no. 5.
              Akademie der Bildenden Künste, Vienna, 1959, no. 3.
              Musée National d'Art Moderne, Paris, 1960-61, no. 482.
              Steinernes Haus, Frankfurt am Main, 1962-63, no. 5.
              Palais de Beaulieu, Lausanne, 1964, no. 200.

31

7

7. THE SHIP OWNER. c. 1889.
    Oil on canvas, 78 x 43¼″ (198 x 110 cm.).
    Signed l. l. "E. Munch".
    Collection Mr. and Mrs. Sigval Bergesen, d. y., Oslo.
    Provenance: Alfred Leonhard Tietz, Cologne.
              K. Doebecke, Berlin.
    Exhibitions: Kunsthütte, Chemnitz, 1929, no. 4.
              Steinernes Haus, Frankfurt am Main, 1962-63, no. 6.

8

8. ARRIVAL OF THE MAIL BOAT. 1890.
   Oil on canvas, 38½ x 51¼″ (98 x 130 cm.).
   Signed and dated l. r. "E. Munch 1890".
   Collection Nicolai A. Andresen, Oslo.
   Provenance: Mrs. Eva Andresen, Oslo.
   Exhibitions: Jeweler Tostrup's Building, Oslo, 1892, no. 45.
   Architektenhaus, Berlin, 1892, no. 33.
   Georg Kleis, Copenhagen, 1893, no. 33.
   Lichtenberg, Dresden, 1893, no. 33.
   Galerie Blanche, Stockholm, 1894, no. 22.
   Steinernes Haus, Frankfurt am Main, 1962-63, no. 3.

9. NIGHT IN ST. CLOUD. 1890.
   Oil on canvas, 25⅜ x 21¼″ (64,5 x 54 cm.).
   Signed l. r. "E. Munch".
   Collection Nasjonalgalleriet, Oslo.
   Provenance: Dr. F. Arentz, Oslo.
   Exhibitions: Jeweler Tostrup's Building, Oslo, 1892, no. 5.
   Architektenhaus, Berlin, 1892, no. 5.
   Georg Kleis, Copenhagen, 1893, no. 5.
   Lichtenberg, Dresden, 1893, no. 5.
   Galerie Blanche, Stockholm, 1894, no. 45.
   Nasjonalgalleriet, Oslo, 1927, no. 40.
   Haus der Kunst, Munich, 1954, no. 15.
   XXVII Biennale, Venice, 1954, no. 9.
   Kunstforeningen, Copenhagen, 1955, no. 14.
   Akademie der Bildenden Künste, Vienna, 1959, no. 4.
   Museum Narodowe, Warsaw, 1959, no. 6.

10

10. RUE LAFAYETTE. 1891.
    Oil on canvas, 36¼ x 28¾" (92 x 73 cm.)
    Signed l. r. "E. Munch 91".
    Collection Nasjonalgalleriet, Oslo.
    Provenance: Thora Lynneberg, Oslo.
    Exhibitions: Jeweler Tostrup's Building, Oslo, 1892, no. 13.
                 Architektenhaus, Berlin, 1892, no. 54.
                 Georg Kleis, Copenhagen, 1893, no. 53.
                 Lichtenberg, Dresden, 1893, no. 51.
                 Galerie Blanche, Stockholm, 1894, no. 1.
                 Dioramalokalet, Oslo, 1900, no. 77.
                 Nasjonalgalleriet, Oslo, 1927, no. 48.
                 The London Gallery, London, 1936.
                 Haus der Kunst, Munich, 1954, no. 16.
                 Kunstforeningen, Copenhagen, 1955, no. 15.
                 Kunstmuseum, Bern, 1958, no. 6.
                 Akademie der Bildenden Künste, Vienna, 1959, no. 6.

11

11. SPRING DAY ON KARL JOHAN STREET, OSLO. 1891.
   Oil on canvas, 31½ x 39½″ (80 x 100 cm.).
   Signed and dated l. l. "E. Munch 91".
   Collection Bergen Billedgalleri, Bergen.
   Provenance: Jens Z. M. Kielland, Stavanger.
              Kunstforening, Bergen.
   Exhibitions: Jeweler Tostrup's Building, Oslo, 1892, no. 22.
              Architektenhaus, Berlin, 1892, no. 28.
              Georg Kleis, Copenhagen, 1893, no. 28.
              Lichtenberg, Dresden, 1893, no. 28.
              Nationalgalerie, Berlin, 1927, no. 22.
              Nasjonalgalleriet, Oslo, 1927, no. 50.
              Institute of Contemporary Art, Boston, 1950, no. 6.
              Edvard Munch, Brighton, 1951, no. 5.
              Gemeentemuseum, The Hague, 1951-52, no. 6.
              Petit Palais, Paris, 1952, no. 5.
              Haus der Kunst, Munich, 1954, no. 18.
              Kunstforeningen, Copenhagen, 1955, no. 17.
              Musée National d'Art Moderne, Paris, 1960-61, no. 483.

12

12. THE KISS. 1892.
    Oil on canvas, 39⅜ x 31¾″ (100 x 80,5 cm.).
    Signed and dated l. r. "E. Munch 92".
    Collection Munch-museet, Oslo.
    Provenance: Gift of the artist.

13

13. EVENING ON KARL JOHAN STREET, OSLO, c. 1892.
   Oil on canvas, 33¼ x 47⅝" (84,5 x 121 cm.).
   Signed l. r. "E. Munch".
   Collection Rasmus Meyers Samlinger, Bergen.
   Provenance: The artist.
   Exhibitions: Blomqvists Lokale, Oslo, 1895.
               Ateneumin Taidemuseo, Helsinki, 1909, no. 28.
               Blomqvists Lokale, Oslo, 1909.
               Nationalgalerie, Berlin, 1927, no. 60.
               Nasjonalgalleriet, Oslo, 1927, no. 91.
               The London Gallery, London, 1936.
               Gemeentemuseum, The Hague, 1949-50, no. 62.
               Palais des Beaux-Arts, Brussels, 1952, no. 53.
               XXVII Biennale, Venice, 1954, no. 13.
               Haus der Kunst, Munich, 1954, no. 20.
               Kunstforeningen, Copenhagen, 1955, no. 19.
               Kunstmuseum, Bern, 1958, no. 9.
               Musée National d'Art Moderne, Paris, 1960-61, no. 484.
               Steinernes Haus, Frankfurt am Main, 1962-63, no. 11.
               Louisiana Museum, Copenhagen, 1963, no. 49.

14

14. MYSTIC SHORE. c. 1892.
   Oil on canvas, 39½ x 55⅛″ (100 x 140 cm.).
   Signed l. r. "E. Munch".
   Collection Haakon Thomas Onstad, Munkedal, Sweden.
   Provenance: Harald Holst Halvorsen, Oslo.
           Dr. Gunnar Johnson Host, Gothenburg.
           Haakon Onstad, Munkedal, Sweden.
   Exhibitions: Jeweler Tostrup's Building, Oslo, 1892, no. 4.
           Architektenhaus, Berlin, 1892, no. 4.
           Georg Kleis, Copenhagen, 1893, no. 4.
           Lichtenberg, Dresden, 1893, no. 4.
           Galerie Blanche, Stockholm, 1894, no. 39.
           Kungl. Akademien, Stockholm, 1941, no. 527.
           Nationalmuseum, Stockholm, 1944, no. 2.
           Steinernes Haus, Frankfurt am Main, 1962-63, no. 10.

15

15. SELF-PORTRAIT BENEATH THE MASK. c. 1892.
    Oil on canvas, 27⅛ x 17⅛″ (69 x 43,5 cm.).
    Not signed or dated.
    Collection Munch-museet, Oslo.
    Provenance: Gift of the artist.
    Exhibitions: Liljevalchs Konsthall, Stockholm, 1947, no. 23.
               Institute of Contemporary Art, Boston, 1950, no. 20.
               Edvard Munch, Brighton, 1951, no. 19.
               Gemeentemuseum, The Hague, 1951-52, no. 20.

16

17

16. PORTRAIT OF DAGNY JUELL PRZYBYSZEWSKA. 1893.
   Oil on canvas, 58¼ x 39¼″ (148,5 x 99,5 cm.).
   Not signed or dated.
   Collection Munch-museet, Oslo.
   Provenance: Gift of the artist.
   Exhibitions: Ugo Barroccio, Berlin, 1893, no. 3.
           Galerie Blanche, Stockholm, 1894, no. 15.
           Blomqvists Lokale, Oslo, 1909.
           Nasjonalgalleriet, Oslo, 1927, no. 71.
           Raadhushallen, Copenhagen, 1946, no. 12.
           Liljevalchs Konsthall, Stockholm, 1947, no. 17.
           Institute of Contemporary Art, Boston, 1950, no. 10.
           Edvard Munch, Brighton, 1951, no. 9.
           Gemeentemuseum, The Hague, 1951-52, no. 10.
           Petit Palais, Paris, 1952, no. 9.
           Museum Narodowe, Warsaw, 1959, no. 7.

17. MOONLIGHT ON THE SHORE. 1893.
   Oil on canvas, 24½ x 37¾″ (62,4 x 95,8 cm.).
   Signed l. r. "E. Munch".
   Collection Rasmus Meyers Samlinger, Bergen.
   Provenance: The artist.
   Exhibitions: Nationalgalerie, Berlin, 1927, no. 37.
           Nasjonalgalleriet, Oslo, 1927, no. 66.
           Haus der Kunst, Munich, 1954, no. 26.

18

19

18. MOONLIGHT. 1893.
   Oil on canvas, 55¼ x 53⅛″ (140,5 x 135 cm.).
   Signed l. r. "E. Munch".
   Collection Nasjonalgalleriet, Oslo.
   Provenance: Harald Nørregaard, Oslo.
   Exhibitions: Ugo Barroccio, Berlin, 1883, no. 18.
            Georg Kleis, Copenhagen, 1893, no. 43.
            Galerie Blanche, Stockholm, 1894, no. 43.
            Arno Wolfframm (Dresdener Kunstsalon), Dresden, 1900, no. 35.
            Dioramalokalet, Oslo, 1904, no. 9.
            Den Norske Kunstudstilling Ved Charlottenberg,
               Copenhagen, 1915, no. 284.
            Nationalgalerie, Berlin, 1927, no. 35.
            Nasjonalgalleriet, Oslo, 1927, no. 64.
            Gemeentemuseum, The Hague, 1949-50, no. 61.
            Palais des Beaux-Arts, Brussels, 1950, no. 54.
            XXVII Biennale, Venice, 1954, no. 15.
            Haus der Kunst, Munich, 1954, no. 25.
            Kunstforeningen, Copenhagen, 1955, no. 25.
            Museum Boymans-van Beuningen, Rotterdam, 1958-59, no. 2.
            Musée National d'Art Moderne, Paris, 1960-61, no. 485.
            Nasjonalgalleriet, Oslo, 1964, no. 54.
            Kunsthalle, Kiel, 1964, no. 55.

19. THE VOICE. 1893.
   Oil on canvas, 34⅝ x 43¼″ (88 x 110 cm.).
   Signed and dated l. l. "E. Munch 1893".
   Collection Museum of Fine Arts, Boston.
   Provenance: Dr. Helge Backstrom, Gothenburg.
            Moderne Galerie Thannhauser, Berlin.
            Harald Holst Halvorsen, Oslo.
   Exhibitions: Dioramalokalet, Oslo, 1897.
            Salong Joël, Stockholm, 1913.
            Kunstnernes Hus, Olso, 1951, no. 54.
            Gemeentemuseum, The Hague, 1951-52, no. 11.
            Kunsthaus, Zürich, 1952, no. 5.
            Kunstmuseum, Bern, 1958, no. 11.

20

20. THE CRY (THE SHRIEK). 1893.
     Oil and tempera on board, 35¾ x 29″ (91 x 73,5 cm.).
     Signed l. l. "E. Munch 1893".
     Collection Nasjonalgalleriet, Oslo.
     Provenance: Gift of Olaf Schou, 1909.
     Exhibitions: Galerie Blanche, Stockholm, 1894, no. 68.
               Ugo Barroccio, Berlin 1895, no. 14.
               Arno Wolfframm (Dresdener Kunstsalon), 1900, no. 26.
               Nasjonalgalleriet, Oslo, 1927, no. 74.
               XXVII Biennale, Venice, 1954, no. 14.
               Haus der Kunst, Munich, 1954, no. 23.
               Kunstforeningen, Copenhagen, 1955, no. 23.
               The Museum of Modern Art, New York, 1960, no. 208.
               Steinernes Haus, Frankfurt am Main, 1962-63, no. 17.
               Louisiana Museum, Copenhagen, 1963, no. 50.
               Zeugnisse der Angst, Darmstadt, 1963.
               Ruhrfestspiele, Recklinghausen, 1965.

21

21. STARRY NIGHT. c. 1893.
   Oil on canvas, 53⅛ x 55⅛″ (135 x 140 cm.).
   Signed l. l. "E. Munch".
   Collection Johan Henrik Andresen, Oslo.
   Provenance: Fridtjof Nansen, Oslo.
               Mrs. Eva Andresen, Oslo.
   Exhibitions: Ugo Barroccio, Berlin, 1893-94, no. 17.
               Galerie Blanche, Stockholm, 1894, no. 42.
               Dioramalokalet, Oslo, 1900, no. 85.
               Hollaendergaarden, Oslo, 1901, no. 67.
               Dioramalokalet, Oslo, 1904, no. 1.
               Ateneumin Taidemuseo, Helsinki, 1909, no. 24.
               The American Art Galleries, New York, 1912, no. 146.
               Künstlerbund Hagen, Vienna, 1912, no. 16.
               Liljevalchs Konsthall, Stockholm, 1917, no. 142.
               Nationalgalerie, Berlin, 1927, no. 36.
               Nasjonalgalleriet, Oslo, 1927, no. 65.
               XXVII Biennale, Venice, 1954, no. 17.
               Haus der Kunst, Munich, 1954, no. 28.
               Palazzo delle Esposizioni, Rome, 1955, no. 4074.
               Kunstmuseum, Bern, 1958, no. 17.
               Kunstnerforbundet, Oslo, 1958, no. 12.
               Museum Narodowe, Warsaw, 1959, no. 6.
               Steinernes Haus, Frankfurt am Main, 1962-63, no. 14.
               Louisiana Museum, Copenhagen, 1963, no. 51.

22

22. VAMPIRE. c. 1893.
        Oil on canvas, 30¼ x 38½″ (77 x 98 cm.).
        Not signed or dated.
        Collection Munch-museet, Oslo.
        Provenance: Gift of the artist.
        Exhibitions: Institute of Contemporary Art, Boston, 1950, no. 12.
                Kunstmuseum, Bern, 1958, no. 14.
                Museum Boymans-van Beuningen, Rotterdam, 1958-59, no. 4.

23

23. MADONNA. 1893-94.
      Oil on canvas, 35½ x 27″ (90 x 68,5 cm.).
      Signed u. l. "E. Munch".
      Collection Munch-museet, Oslo.
      Provenance: Gift of the artist.
      Exhibitions: Raadhushallen, Copenhagen, 1946, no. 17.
                          Liljevalchs Konsthall, Stockholm, 1947, no. 19.
                          Institute of Contemporary Art, Boston, 1950, no. 13.
                          Edvard Munch, Brighton, 1951, no. 12.
                          Gemeentemuseum, The Hague, 1951-52, no. 13.
                          Petit Palais, Paris, 1952, no. 12.

24

24. ROSE AND AMÉLIE. 1894.
   Oil on canvas, 30¾ x 42⅞″ (78 x 109 cm.).
   Signed u. l. "E. Munch 94".
   Collection Munch-museet, Olso (Deposit of the Aker-Collection, Oslo).
   Provenance: Rolf E. Stenersen, Oslo.
   Exhibitions: *Salon des Indépendants*, Paris, 1896.

25

25. JEALOUSY. 1894-95.
    Oil on canvas, 26¼ x 39½″ (66,8 x 100 cm.).
    Signed l. r. "E. M. 9-?".
    Collection Rasmus Meyers Samlinger, Bergen.
    Provenance: The artist.
    Exhibitions: Ugo Barroccio, Berlin, 1895, no. 11.
               Blomqvists Lokale, Oslo, 1895-96.
               Dioramalokalet, Oslo, 1900, no. 43.
               Arno Wolfframm (Dresdener Kunstsalon), Dresden, 1900, no. 39.
               Secession, Berlin, 1902, no. 196.
               Dioramalokalet, Oslo, 1904, no. 12.
               Galerie "Mánes", Prague, 1905, no. 36.
               Sonderbund, Cologne, 1912, no. 527.
               Nationalgalerie, Berlin, 1927, no. 53.
               Gemeentemuseum, The Hague, 1949-50, no. 59.
               Institute of Contemporary Art, Boston, 1950, no. 19.
               Edvard Munch, Brighton, 1951, no. 18.
               Gemeentemuseum, The Hague, 1951-52, no. 19.
               Palais des Beaux-Arts, Brussels, 1952, no. 6.
               Kunsthaus, Zürich, 1952, no. 15.
               Haus der Kunst, Munich, 1954.
               Kunstforeningen, Copenhagen, 1955, no. 13.
               Kunstmuseum, Bern, 1958, no. 26.
               Museum Narodowe, Warsaw, 1959, no. 5.
               Louisiana Museum, Copenhagen, 1963, no. 53.
               Haus der Kunst, Munich, 1964, no. 388.

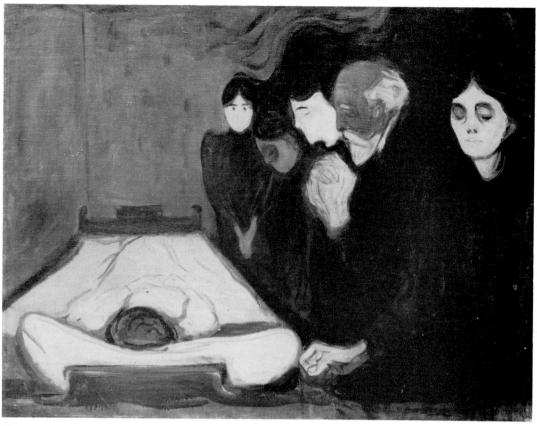

26

26. THE DEATH BED. 1895.
   Oil on canvas, 36¼ x 47½″ (90,2 x 120,5 cm.).
   Signed l. l. "E. Munch".
   Collection Rasmus Meyers Samlinger, Bergen.
   Provenance: The artist.
   Exhibitions: Dioramalokalet, Oslo, 1900, no. 13.
            Dioramalokalet, Oslo, 1904, no. 18.
            Blomqvists Lokale, Oslo, 1909.
            Nationalgalerie, Berlin, 1927, no. 56.
            Nasjonalgalleriet, Oslo, 1927, no. 87.
            Institute of Contemporary Art, Boston, 1950, no. 18.
            Edvard Munch, Brighton, 1951, no. 17.
            Gemeentemuseum, The Hague, 1951-52, no. 18.
            Petit Palais, Paris, 1952, no. 17.
            Kunsthaus, Zürich, 1952, no. 16.
            XXVII Biennale, Venice, 1954, no. 21.
            Haus der Kunst, Munich, 1954, no. 35.
            Kunstforeningen, Copenhagen, 1955, no. 33.
            Museum Narodowe, Warsaw, 1959, no. 11.
            Haus der Kunst, Munich, 1964, no. 390.

27. MOTHER AND DAUGHTER. 1897.
   Oil on canvas, 53⅛ x 64⅛″ (135 x 163 cm.).
   Not signed or dated.
   Collection Nasjonalgalleriet, Oslo.
   Provenance: Gift of Olaf Schou, Oslo, 1896.
   Exhibitions: Nasjonalgalleriet, Oslo, 1927, no. 109.
            London Gallery, London, 1936.
            Haus der Kunst, Munich, 1954, no. 38.
            Kunstforeningen, Copenhagen, 1955, no. 36.
            Kunstmuseum, Bern, 1958, no. 28.

28. THE RED VINE. 1898. (Illustration page 17)
    Oil on canvas, 47 x 47⅝″ (119,5 x 121 cm.).
    Signed u. l. "E. Munch".
    Collection Munch-museet, Oslo.
    Provenance: Gift of the artist.
    Exhibitions: Arno Wolfframm (Dresdener Kunstsalon), Dresden, 1900, no. 27.
               Dioramalokalet, Oslo, 1910, no. 5.
               Liljevalchs Konsthall, Stockholm, 1947, no. 33.
               Institute of Contemporary Art, Boston, 1950, no. 27.
               Edvard Munch, Brighton, 1951, no. 26.
               Gemeentemuseum, The Hague, 1951-52, no. 27.
               Petit Palais, Paris, 1952, no. 26.

29. FERTILITY. c. 1898.
    Oil on canvas, 48 x 56¾″ (122 x 144 cm.).
    Signed l. l. "E. Munch".
    Collection Mr. and Mrs. Sigval Bergesen, d.y., Oslo.
    Provenance: Dr. Max Linde, Lübeck.
               Christian Langaard, Oslo.
               Heggtveit, Stange, Norway.
               P. M. Røwde, Oslo.
    Exhibitions: Secession, Vienna, 1903-04, no. 50.
               Kunsthalle, Mannheim, 1926-27, no. 9.
               Nasjonalgalleriet, Oslo, 1927, no. 280.
               Kunstnernes Hus, Oslo, 1948, no. 70.
               Kunstnerforbundet, Oslo, 1961, no. 16.
               Steinernes Haus, Frankfurt am Main, 1962-63, no. 21.
               Nasjonalgalleriet, Oslo, 1964, no. 55.
               Kunsthalle, Kiel, 1964, no. 58.

29

31

30. MELANCHOLY. 1899.
   Oil on canvas, 43¼ x 49⅝″ (110 x 126 cm.).
   Not signed or dated.
   Collection Munch-museet, Oslo.
   Provenance: Gift of the artist.
   Exhibitions: Grossherzogliches Museum, Weimar, 1906.
           Fischer, Bielefeld, 1907.
           Konstnärshuset, Stockholm, 1913, no. 26.
           Galerie Fritz Gurlitt, Berlin, 1914, no. 38.
           Nationalgalerie, Berlin, 1927, no. 65.
           Nasjonalgalleriet, Oslo, 1927, no. 113.
           International Exhibition, Dresden, 1926, no. 241.
           Kunsthalle, Mannheim, 1926-27, no. 6.
           Raadhushallen, Copenhagen, 1946, no. 24.
           Liljevalchs Konsthall, Stockholm, 1947, no. 32.
           Institute of Contemporary Art, Boston, 1950, no. 28.
           Edvard Munch, Brighton, 1951, no. 27.
           Gemeentemuseum, The Hague, 1951-52, no. 28.
           Petit Palais, Paris, 1952, no. 27.
           Kunstmuseum, Bern, 1958, no. 30.
           Museum Boymans-van Beuningen, Rotterdam, 1958-59, no. 13.
           Akademie der Bildenden Künste, Vienna, 1959, no. 18.

31. THE DANCE OF LIFE. 1899-1900.
   Oil on canvas, 49½ x 75″ (125,5 x 190,5 cm.).
   Signed and dated l. l. "E. Munch 99", u. r. "E. Munch 1900".
   Collection Nasjonalgalleriet, Oslo.
   Provenance: Gift of Olaf Schou, 1909.
   Exhibitions: Secession, Berlin, 1902, no. 190.
           Dioramalokalet, Oslo, 1904, no. 11.
           Dioramalokalet, Oslo, 1910, no. 51.
           Blomqvists Lokale, Oslo, 1918, no. 10.
           Nationalgalerie, Berlin, 1927, no. 58.
           Nasjonalgalleriet, Oslo, 1927, no. 89.
           Institute of Contemporary Art, Boston, 1950, no. 25.
           Edvard Munch, Brighton, 1951, no. 24.
           Petit Palais, Paris, 1952, no. 24.
           Gemeentemuseum, The Hague, 1951-52, no. 25.
           Palais des Beaux-Arts, Brussels, 1952, no. 9.
           Kunsthaus, Zürich, 1952, no. 18.
           Palais International des Beaux-Arts, Brussels, 1958, no. 240.
           Akademie der Bildenden Künste, Vienna, 1959, no. 16.

32

32. TRAIN SMOKE. c. 1900.
   Oil on canvas, 33½ x 42⅞″ (85 x 109 cm.).
   Signed l. r. "E. Munch".
   Collection Jørgen W. Cappelen, Oslo.
   Provenance: Rasmus Meyer, Bergen.
   Exhibitions: Galerie "Mánes", Prague, 1905.
             Moderne Galerie Thannhauser, Munich, 1912.
             Institute of Contemporary Art, Boston, 1950, no. 31.
             Edvard Munch, Brighton, 1951, no. 30.
             Gemeentemuseum, The Hague, 1951-52, no. 31.
             Steinernes Haus, Frankfurt am Main, 1962-63, no. 24.
             Kunsthalle, Kiel, 1964, no. 60.

33. PORTRAIT OF CONSUL CHRISTEN SANDBERG. 1901.
   Oil on canvas, 93 x 57¾″ (215 x 147 cm.).
   Signed u. r. "E. Munch".
   Collection Munch-museet, Oslo.
   Provenance: Gift of the artist.
   Exhibitions: Hollaendergaarden, Oslo, 1901, no. 61.
             Blomqvists Lokale, Oslo, 1903, no. 34.
             Dioramalokalet, Oslo, 1904, no. 48.
             Galerie "Mánes", Prague, 1905, no. 115.
             Ateneumin Taidemuseo, Helsinki, 1909, no. 21.
             Dioramalokalet, Oslo, 1911, no. 86.
             Sonderbund, Cologne, 1912, no. 528.
             Moderne Galerie Thannhauser, Munich, 1912, no. 7.
             Konstnärshuset, Stockholm, 1913, no. 8.
             Galerie Alfred Flechtheim, Düsseldorf, 1914, no. 19.
             Galerie Fritz Gurlitt, Berlin, 1914, no. 3.
             Nationalgalerie, Berlin, 1927, no. 69.
             Nasjonalgalleriet, Oslo, 1927, no. 118.
             Norwegian Exhibition, London, 1928, no. 133.
             Stedelijk Museum, Amsterdam, 1937, no. 12.
             Kungl. Akademien, Stockholm, 1937, no. 21.
             Palais des Beaux-Arts, Brussels, 1950, no. 52.
             Kunsthaus, Zürich, 1952, no. 25.
             Palais des Beaux-Arts, Brussels, 1952, no. 12.

33

34

34. MIDSUMMER NIGHT. 1901-02.
Oil on canvas, 31⅞ x 29⅛″ (81 x 74 cm.).
Collection A. Fredrik Klaveness, Oslo.
Provenance: Anton Fredrik Klaveness, Oslo.
Exhibitions: Dioramalokalet, Oslo, 1911, no. 38.
Steinernes Haus, Frankfurt am Main, 1962-63, no. 27.

35

35. GROUP OF FOUR GIRLS AT ÅSGÅRDSTRAND. 1902.
     Oil on canvas, 35¼ x 49¼″ (89,5 x 125,5 cm.).
     Signed u. r. "E. Munch".
     Collection Staatsgalerie, Stuttgart.

36

36. THE BEAST (FEMALE NUDE). 1902.
      Oil on canvas, 37¼ x 25″ (94,5 x 63,5 cm.).
      Signed l. r. "E. Munch".
      Collection Städt. Galerie im Landesmuseum, Hannover.
      Provenance: Bernhard Köhler, Berlin.
      Exhibitions: Nationalgalerie, Berlin, 1927, no. 75.
              Nasjonalgalleriet, Oslo, 1927, no. 129.
              Ausstellung Edvard Munch, Cologne, Hamburg, Lübeck, 1951, no. 8.
              Haus der Kunst, Munich, 1954, no. 50.
              Steinernes Haus, Frankfurt am Main, 1962-63, no. 26.

37

37. PORTRAIT OF HARRY GRAF KESSLER. 1904.
    Oil on canvas, 33½ x 29½″ (85 x 75 cm.).
    Signed and dated u. r. "E. Munch 1904".
    Collection Mr. and Mrs. Sigval Bergesen, d.y., Oslo.
    Provenance: Harry Graf Kessler, Weimar.
             Wilhelmine, Marquise de Brion, Paris.
             Comtesse de Brion, Paris.
    Exhibitions: Städtische Kunsthalle, Mannheim, 1926-27, no. 18.
             Nationalgalerie, Berlin, 1927, no. 85.
             Nasjonalgalleriet, Oslo, 1927, no. 134.
             Steinernes Haus, Frankfurt am Main, 1962-63, no. 33.

38

39

38. GIRL UNDER APPLE TREE. 1904.
   Oil on canvas, 43¾ x 39½″ (111 x 100,5 cm.).
   Not signed or dated.
   Collection Museum of Art, Carnegie Institute, Pittsburgh. Acquired through the
      generosity of Mrs. Alan M. Scaife and family.
   Provenance: H. Nobel Roede, Oslo.
      National Gallery, Breslau.
      Nasjonalgalleriet, Oslo, 1939-45 (on deposit).
      Ragnar Moltzau, Oslo, 1945.
      Marlborough-Gerson Gallery, New York.
   Exhibitions: Dioramalokalet, Oslo, 1911, no. 59.
      National Gallery, Breslau, 1927, no. 86.
      Nasjonalgalleriet, Oslo, 1927, no. [136].
      Kunsthütte, Chemnitz, 1929, no. 23.
      Kunsthaus, Zürich, 1952, no. 32.
      Nationalmuseum, Stockholm, 1956, no. 82.
      Kunsthaus, Zürich, 1957, no. 62.
      Gemeentemuseum, The Hague, 1957, no. 63.
      Kunstmuseum, Bern, 1958, no. 45.
      Museum Boymans-van Beuningen, Rotterdam, 1958-59, no. 17a.
      Marlborough-Gerson Gallery, New York, 1963, no. 282.
      The Solomon R. Guggenheim Museum, New York, 1964.

39. DANCE ON THE SHORE. c. 1904.
   Oil on canvas, 39 x 37¾″ (99 x 96 cm.).
   Signed l. l. "E. Munch".
   Collection Národní Galerie, Prague.
   Provenance: Stanislav Sucharda .
      Dr. Palkovsky.
   Exhibition: Galerie "Mánes", Prague, 1905, no. 47.

40

40. DEATH OF MARAT. 1905-27.
   Oil on canvas, 59 x 78¾″ (150 x 200 cm.).
   Not signed or dated.
   Collection Munch-museet, Oslo.
   Provenance: Gift of the artist.
   Exhibitions: Raadhushallen, Copenhagen, 1946, no. 32.
            Liljevalchs Konsthall, Stockholm, 1947, no. 48.
            Institute of Contemporary Art, Boston, no. 39.
            Edvard Munch, Brighton, 1951, no. 38.
            Gemeentemuseum, The Hague, 1952, no. 39.
            Petit Palais, Paris, 1952, no. 36.
            XXVII Biennale, Venice, 1954, no. 27.
            Haus der Kunst, Munich, 1954, no. 68.
            Palazzo delle Esposizioni, Rome, 1955, no. 4076.
            Kunstmuseum, Bern, 1958, no. 53.
            Akademie der Bildenden Künste, Vienna, 1959, no. 41.

41

41. VILLAGE STREET, ELGERSBURG (BOYS, GIRLS AND DUCKS). 1905-37.
   Oil on canvas, 39½ x 41⅜″ (100 x 105 cm.).
   Not signed or dated.
   Collection Munch-museet, Oslo.
   Provenance: Gift of the artist.
   Exhibitions: Kungl. Akademien, Stockholm, 1937, no. 22.
             Stedelijk Museum, Amsterdam, 1937, no. 22.
             Harald Holst Halvorsen, Oslo, 1938, no. 2.
             Liljevalchs Konsthall, Stockholm, 1947, no. 39.
             Institute of Contemporary Art, Boston, 1950, no. 34.
             Edvard Munch, Brighton, 1951, no. 33.
             Gemeentemuseum, The Hague, 1951-52, no. 34.
             Petit Palais, Paris, 1952, no. 31.
             Museum Narodowe, Warsaw, 1959, no. 18.

42

42. AVENUE IN SNOW, KOESEN. 1906.
   Oil on canvas, 31½ x 39½″ (80 x 100 cm.).
   Signed l. l. "E. Munch".
   Collection Munch-museet, Oslo.
   Provenance: Gift of the artist.
   Exhibitions: Nationalgalerie, Berlin, 1927, no. 105.
       Nasjonalgalleriet, Oslo, 1927, no. 154.
       Raadhushallen, Copenhagen, 1946, no. 26.
       Liljevalchs Konsthall, Stockholm, 1947, no. 47.

43. SELF-PORTRAIT WITH WINE BOTTLE. 1906.
   Oil on canvas, 43½ x 47⅜″ (110,5 x 120,5 cm.).
   Signed and dated u. l. "E. Munch 1906".
   Collection Munch-museet, Oslo.
   Provenance: Gift of the artist.
   Exhibitions: Dioramalokalet, Oslo, 1910, no. 52.
       Dioramalokalet, Oslo, 1911, no. 111.
       Künstlerbund Hagen, Vienna, 1912, no. 38.
       Konstnärshuset, Stockholm, 1913, no. 14.
       Galerie Alfred Flechtheim, Düsseldorf, 1914.
       Galerie Fritz Gurlitt, Berlin, 1914, no. 12.
       Konsthallen, Gothenburg, 1923, no. 192.
       Städtische Kunsthalle, Mannheim, 1926-27, no. 33.
       Nationalgalerie, Berlin, 1927, no. 106.
       Nasjonalgalleriet, Oslo, 1927, no. 158.
       Kungl. Akademien, Stockholm, 1937, no. 14.
       Stedelijk Museum, Amsterdam, 1937, no. 18.
       Raadhushallen, Copenhagen, 1946, no. 33.
       Liljevalchs Konsthall, Stockholm, 1947, no. 49.
       Institute of Contemporary Art, Boston, 1950, no. 38.
       Edvard Munch, Brighton, 1951, no. 37.
       Gemeentemuseum, The Hague, 1951-52, no. 38.
       Petit Palais, Paris, 1952, no. 35.
       Kunstmuseum, Bern, 1958, no. 54.
       Museum Boymans-van Beuningen, Rotterdam, 1958-59, no. 20.
       Museum voor Stadt en Lande, Groningen, 1959, no. 3.
       Akademie der Bildenden Künste, Vienna, 1959, no. 38.

43

44

44. CUPID AND PSYCHE. 1907.
    Oil on canvas, 47 x 39″ (119,5 x 99 cm.).
    Signed and dated u. r. "E. Munch 1907".
    Collection Munch-museet, Oslo.
    Provenance: Gift of the artist.
    Exhibitions: Dioramalokalet, Oslo, 1910, no. 65.
            Sonderbund, Cologne, 1912, no. 546.
            Künstlerbund Hagen, Vienna, 1912, no. 43.
            Konstnärshuset, Stockholm, 1913, no. 23.
            Galerie Fritz Gurlitt, Berlin, 1914, no. 79.
            Nationalgalerie, Berlin, 1927, no. 119.
            Nasjonalgalleriet, Oslo, 1927, no. 172.
            Raadhushallen, Copenhagen, 1946, no. 39.
            Liljevalchs Konsthall, Stockholm, 1947, no. 56.

45. PORTRAIT OF WALTER RATHENAU. 1907.
    Oil on canvas, 86⅞ x 43¼″ (220 x 110 cm.).
    Signed l. l. "E. Munch".
    Collection Rasmus Meyers Samlinger, Bergen.
    Provenance: The artist.
    Exhibitions: Secession, Berlin, 1908, no. 183.
            Blomqvists Lokale, Oslo, 1909.
            Nasjonalgalleriet, Oslo, 1927, no. 163.
            Stedelijk Museum, Amsterdam, 1937, no. 21.
            Kungl. Akademien, Stockholm, 1937, no. 65.
            Gemeentemuseum, The Hague, 1949-50.
            Institute of Contemporary Art, Boston, 1950-51, no. 41.
            Edvard Munch, Brighton, 1951, no. 40.
            Gemeentemuseum, The Hague, 1951-52, no. 41.
            Petit Palais, Paris, 1952, no. 38.
            Haus der Kunst, Munich, 1954, no. 69.
            Kunstforeningen, Copenhagen, 1955, no. 44.
            Stedelijk Museum, Amsterdam, 1957, no. 86.

45

46

47

46. THE BATHERS (CENTER SECTION OF TRIPTYCH). 1907-08.
Oil on canvas, 81⅜ x 89½″ (206 x 227 cm.).
Signed and dated l. r. "E. Munch Warnemünde 1907-08".
Collection Ateneumin Taidemuseo, Helsinki.
Provenance: The artist.
Exhibitions: Ateneumin Taidemuseo, Helsinki, 1911.
　　　　　　Sonderbund, Cologne, 1912, no. 543.
　　　　　　Kungl. Akademien, Stockholm, 1937, no. 72.
　　　　　　Steinernes Haus, Frankfurt am Main, 1962-63, no. 41.

47. ADAM AND EVE UNDER THE APPLE TREE. 1908.
Oil on canvas, 51¼ x 79½″ (130,5 x 202 cm.).
Signed u. r. "E. Munch 1908".
Collection Munch-museet, Oslo.
Provenance: Gift of the artist.
Exhibitions: Sonderbund, Cologne, 1912, no. 248.
　　　　　　The American-Scandinavian Society,
　　　　　　　New York, 1912-13, no. 147.
　　　　　　Liljevalchs Konsthall, Stockholm, 1917, no. 148.
　　　　　　Raadhushallen, Copenhagen, 1946, no. 43.
　　　　　　Liljevalchs Konsthall, Stockholm, 1947, no. 42.
　　　　　　Institute of Contemporary Art, Boston, 1950, no. 37.
　　　　　　Edvard Munch, Brighton, 1951, no. 36.
　　　　　　Gemeentemuseum, The Hague, 1952, no. 34.
　　　　　　Petit Palais, Paris, 1952, no. 34.

48

48. TWO PEOPLE ON THE SHORE (THE SOLITARY ONES). 1908.
   Oil on canvas, 31⅞ x 43¼″ (81 x 110 cm.).
   Signed and dated u. r. "E. Munch 1908".
   Private Collection, Oslo.
   Provenance: H. Nobel Roede, Oslo.
              Städtische Kunstsammlung, Chemnitz.
   Exhibitions: Ateneumin Taidemuseo, Helsinki, 1909, no. 9.
              Nationalgalerie, Berlin, 1927, no. 127.
              Nasjonalgalleriet, Oslo, 1927, no. 182.
              Kunsthütte, Chemnitz, 1929, no. 34.
              London Gallery, London, 1936.
              Kunstnernes Hus, Oslo, 1951, no. 77.
              Kunstnerforbundet, Oslo, 1958, no. 22.
              Steinernes Haus, Frankfurt am Main, 1962-63, no. 42.

49

49. MASON AND MECHANIC. 1908.
      Oil on canvas, 35⅜ x 27⅜″ (90 x 69,5 cm.).
      Signed l. l. "E. Munch".
      Collection Munch-museet, Oslo.
      Provenance: Gift of the artist.
      Exhibitions: Dioramalokalet, Oslo, 1911, no. 43.
                        Nasjonalgalleriet, Oslo, 1927, no. 277.
                        Harald Holst Halvorsen, Oslo, 1938, no. 13.
                        Raadhushallen, Copenhagen, 1946, no. 40.
                        Liljevalchs Konsthall, Stockholm, 1947, no. 59.
                        Institute of Contemporary Art, Boston, 1950, no. 42.
                        Edvard Munch, Brighton, 1951, no. 41.
                        Gemeentemuseum, The Hague, 1951-52, no. 42.
                        Petit Palais, Paris, 1952, no. 39.

50

50. PORTRAIT OF DR. DANIEL JACOBSON. 1909.
   Oil on canvas, 80½ x 43⅞″ (204 x 111,5 cm.).
   Signed and dated u. l. "Edv. Munch Kjøbenhavn 1909".
   Collection Munch-museet, Oslo.
   Provenance: Gift of the artist.
   Exhibitions: Blomqvists Lokale, Oslo, 1909.
              Sonderbund, Cologne, 1912, no. 549.
              Moderne Galerie Thannhauser, Munich, 1912, no. 5.
              Konstnärshuset, Stockholm, 1913, no. 5.
              Galerie Fritz Gurlitt, Berlin, 1914, no. 42.
              Den Norske Kunstudstilling Ved Charlottenberg,
                Copenhagen, 1915, no. 275.
              Kunsthaus, Zürich, 1922, no. 35.
              Konsthallen, Gothenburg, 1923, no. 173.
              Nasjonalgalleriet, Oslo, 1927, no. 186.
              Raadhushallen, Copenhagen, 1946, no. 44.
              Liljevalchs Konsthall, Stockholm, 1947, no. 67.
              Institute of Contemporary Art, Boston, 1950, no. 46.
              Edvard Munch, Brighton, 1951, no. 45.
              Gemeentemuseum, The Hague, 1951-52, no. 46.
              Petit Palais, Paris, 1952, no. 43.
              XXVII Biennale, Venice, 1954, no. 29.
              Haus der Kunst, Munich, 1954, no. 43.
              Kunstforeningen, Copenhagen, 1955, no. 46.
              Palazzo delle Esposizioni, Rome, 1955, no. 4077.
              Kunstmuseum, Bern, 1958, no. 63.
              Museum Boymans-van Beuningen,
                Rotterdam, 1958-59, no. 21.
              Akademie der Bildenden Künste,
                Vienna, 1959, no. 46.

51. PORTRAIT OF THE NOTARY TORVALD STANG. 1909.
   Oil on canvas, 79¾ x 38″ (202 x 96,5 cm.).
   Signed and dated u. r. "E. Munch 1908" and u. l. "E. Munch 1909".
   Collection Munch-museet, Oslo.
   Provenance: Gift of the artist.
   Exhibitions: Sonderbund, Cologne, 1912, no. 547.
              Konstnärshuset, Stockholm, 1913, no. 3.
              Nationalgalerie, Berlin, 1927, no. 130.
              Liljevalchs Konsthall, Stockholm, 1947, no. 69.
              Institute of Contemporary Art, Boston, 1950, no. 47.
              Edvard Munch, Brighton, 1951, no. 46.
              Gemeentemuseum, The Hague, 1951-52, no. 47.
              Petit Palais, Paris, 1952, no. 44.
              XXVII Biennale, Venice, 1954, no. 30.
              Haus der Kunst, Munich, 1954, no. 75.
              Kunstforeningen, Copenhagen, 1955, no. 48.

51

52

52. SELF-PORTRAIT IN A BLUE SUIT. 1909.
   Oil on canvas, 39½ x 43½″ (100 x 110 cm.).
   Signed and dated u. r. "E. Munch Kjøbenhavn 1909".
   Collection Rasmus Meyers Samlinger, Bergen.
   Provenance: The artist.
   Exhibitions: Blomqvists Lokale, Oslo, 1909.
             Nationalgalerie, Berlin, 1927, no. 129.
             Nasjonalgalleriet, Oslo, 1927, no. 184.
             Palais des Beaux-Arts, Brussels, 1950, no. 58.
             Haus der Kunst, Munich, 1954, no. 73.
             Kunstforeningen, Copenhagen, 1955, no. 47.
             Kunstmuseum, Bern, 1958, no. 60.

53

53. BOY IN BLUE (STUDY FOR THE MURAL "HISTORY"). c. 1909.
   Oil on canvas, 30½ x 26⅛″ (77,5 x 66,3 cm.).
   Signed l. r. "E. Munch".
   Collection The Detroit Institute of Arts.
   Provenance: A. Flechtheim, Berlin.
   Exhibitions: M. H. de Young Memorial Museum, San Francisco, 1945.
                Allen Memorial Art Museum, Oberlin College, Oberlin, Ohio, 1946, no. 2.
                University of Minnesota Art Gallery, Minneapolis, January 28-March 7, 1952.

54. GALLOPING HORSE. 1912.
    Oil on canvas, 58¼ x 47″ (148 x 119,5 cm.).
    Signed u. r. "E. Munch".
    Collection Munch-museet, Oslo.
    Provenance: Gift of the artist.
    Exhibitions: Konstnärshuset, Stockholm, 1913, no. 30.
              Galerie Fritz Gurlitt, Berlin, 1914, no. 1.
              Nationalgalerie, Berlin, 1927, no. 148.
              Nasjonalgalleriet, Oslo, 1927, no. 195.
              Norwegian Exhibition, London, 1928, no. 136.
              Kunsthaus, Zürich, 1932, no. 13.
              Kungl. Akademien, Stockholm, 1937, no. 29.
              Stedelijk Museum, Amsterdam, 1937, no. 33.
              Nasjonalgalleriet, Oslo, 1940, no. 322.
              Raadhushallen, Copenhagen, 1946, no. 51.
              Liljevalchs Konsthall, Stockholm, 1947, no. 80.
              Institute of Contemporary Art, Boston, 1950, no. 49.
              Edvard Munch, Brighton, 1951, no. 48.
              Gemeentemuseum, The Hague, 1951-52, no. 49.
              Petit Palais, Paris, 1952, no. 48.
              XXVII Biennale, Venice, 1954, no. 32.
              Haus der Kunst, Munich, 1954, no. 80.
              Palazzo delle Esposizioni, Rome, 1955, no. 4079.

55

55. WINTER, KRAGERØ. 1912.
   Oil on canvas, 52 x 51½″ (132 x 131 cm.).
   Signed and dated l. l. "E. Munch 1912".
   Collection Munch-museet, Oslo.
   Provenance: Gift of the artist.
   Exhibitions: Nationalgalerie, Berlin, 1927, no. 151.
   Nasjonalgalleriet, Oslo, 1927, no. 197.
   Raadhushallen, Copenhagen, 1946, no. 52.
   Liljevalchs Konsthall, Stockholm, 1947, no. 80.
   Institute of Contemporary Art, Boston, 1950, no. 48.
   Edvard Munch, Brighton, 1951, no. 47.
   Gemeentemuseum, The Hague, 1951-52, no. 48.
   Petit Palais, Paris, 1952, no. 47.

56. WORKMEN ON THEIR WAY HOME. 1915.
   Oil on canvas, 49⅜ x 89½″ (201 x 227 cm.).
   Not signed or dated.
   Collection Munch-museet, Oslo.
   Provenance: Gift of the artist.
   Exhibitions: Blomqvists Lokale, Oslo, 1918, no. 37.
   Kunsthaus, Zürich, 1922, no. 47.
   Nasjonalgalleriet, Oslo, 1927, no. 289.
   Liljevalchs Konsthall, Stockholm, 1947, no. 92.
   Institute of Contemporary Art, Boston, 1950, no. 51.
   Edvard Munch, Brighton, 1951, no. 50.
   Gemeentemuseum, The Hague, 1951-52, no. 51.
   Petit Palais, Paris, 1952, no. 50.
   Kunsthaus, Zürich, 1952, no. 57.
   Palais des Beaux-Arts, Brussels, 1952, no. 16.
   Kunstnerforbundet, Oslo, 1957, no. 26.
   Palais des Expositions, Charleroi, 1958, no. 80.

57

57. WINTER, KRAGERØ. 1915.
  Oil on canvas, 54¾ x 68″ (139 x 173 cm.).
  Signed and dated l. r. "E. Munch 1915".
  Collection Mr. and Mrs. Nils Astrup, Oslo.
  Provenance: J. B. Stang, Oslo.
  Exhibitions: Nationalgalerie, Berlin, 1927, no. 169.
        Nasjonalgalleriet, Oslo, 1927, no. 216.
        Kunstnernes Hus, Oslo, 1951, no. 81.

58. GIRL SEATED ON THE EDGE OF HER BED. 1915-16.
  Oil on canvas, 55½ x 41¾″ (141 x 106 cm.).
  Signed l. l. "E. Munch".
  Collection Nationalmuseum, Stockholm.
  Provenance: The artist, 1917.
  Exhibitions: Liljevalchs Konsthall, Stockholm, 1917, no. 162.
        Nasjonalgalleriet, Oslo, 1927, no. 233.
        Nationalmuseum, Stockholm, 1944, no. 32.

59

59. MAN IN A CABBAGE FIELD. 1916.
   Oil on canvas, 53½ x 71¼″ (136 x 181 cm.).
   Signed l. l. "E. Munch 16".
   Collection Nasjonalgalleriet, Oslo.
   Provenance: Gift of Christian Mustad.
   Exhibitions: Georg Kleis, Copenhagen, 1917, no. 23.
               Kunsthaus, Zürich, 1922, no. 52.
               Konsthallen, Gothenburg, 1923, no. 193.
               Nationalgalerie, Berlin, 1927, no. 172.
               Nasjonalgalleriet, Oslo, 1927, no. 222.
               Palais des Beaux-Arts, Brussels, 1952, no. 17.
               Kunsthaus, Zürich, 1952, no. 17.

60

60. PEASANT WITH HORSE. 1918.
    Oil on canvas, 51⅛ x 59″ (130 x 150 cm.).
    Signed and dated l. r. "E. Munch 1918".
    Collection Haakon Thomas Onstad, Munkedal, Sweden.
    Provenance: Pinakothek, Munich.
                 Haakon Onstad, Munkedal, Sweden.
    Exhibitions: Harald Holst Halvorsen, Oslo, 1938.
               Kunsthaus, Zürich, 1952, no. 63.
               Steinernes Haus, Frankfurt am Main, 1962-63, no. 51.

61

61. STARRY NIGHT. 1923-24.
    Oil on canvas, 47½ x 39⅜″ (120,5 x 100 cm.).
    Not signed or dated.
    Collection Munch-museet, Oslo.
    Provenance: Gift of the artist.
    Exhibitions: Liljevalchs Konsthall, Stockholm, 1947, no. 120.
               Institute of Contemporary Art, Boston, 1950, no. 56.
               XXVII Biennale, Venice, 1954, no. 38.

62

62. SEATED MODEL. 1925-28.
Oil on canvas, 53¾ x 45½″ (136,5 x 115,5 cm.).
Signed and dated l. r. "E. Munch 1928".
Collection Munch-museet, Oslo.
Provenance: Gift of the artist.
Exhibitions: Nationalgalerie, Berlin, 1927, no. 209.
Nasjonalgalleriet, Oslo, 1927, no. 265.
Kungl. Akademien, Stockholm, 1937, no. 54.
Stedelijk Museum, Amsterdam, 1937, no. 56.
Liljevalchs Konsthall, Stockholm, 1947, no. 137.
Institute of Contemporary Art, Boston, 1950, no. 58.
Edvard Munch, Brighton, 1951, no. 57.
Gemeentemuseum, The Hague, 1951-52, no. 58.
Petit Palais, Paris, 1952, no. 57.
Kunsthaus, Zürich, 1952, no. 75.
Palais des Beaux-Arts, Brussels, 1952, no. 22.
XXVII Biennale, Venice, 1954, no. 41.
Haus der Kunst, Munich, 1954, no. 98.
Kunstforeningen, Copenhagen, 1955, no. 58.

63

63. SELF-PORTRAIT WITH PALETTE. 1926.
   Oil on canvas, 35⅜ x 26¾″ (90 x 68 cm.).
   Not signed or dated.
   Private Collection, Oslo.
   Provenance: Kunsthalle, Mannheim.
              Harald Holst Halvorsen, Oslo.
   Exhibitions: Städtische Kunsthalle, Mannheim, 1926-27, no. 72.
              Nationalgalerie, Berlin, 1927, no. 214.
              Nasjonalgalleriet, Oslo, 1927, no. 272.
              Kunsthütte, Chemnitz, 1929, no. 55.
              Kunstverein, Leipzig, 1929, no. 46.
              Kunsthaus, Zürich, 1932, no. 35.
              Harald Holst Halvorsen, Oslo, 1938, no. 34.
              Kunsthaus, Zürich, 1952, no. 74.
              XXVII Biennale, Venice, 1954, no. 40.
              Haus der Kunst, Munich, 1954, no. 97.
              Kunstforeningen, Copenhagen, 1955, no. 58.
              Kunstnerforbundet, Oslo, 1958, no. 42.
              Museum Narodowe, Warsaw, 1959, no. 22.

64

64. THE SICK CHILD. c. 1927.
   Oil on canvas, 46 x 45¾″ (117 x 116 cm.).
   Signed u. r. "E. Munch".
   Collection Munch-museet, Oslo.
   Provenance: Gift of the artist.
   Exhibitions: Institute of Contemporary Art, Boston, 1950, no. 57.
      Edvard Munch, Brighton, 1951, no. 56.
      Gemeentemuseum, The Hague, 1951-52, no. 57.
      Petit Palais, Paris, 1952, no. 55.
      Kunstmuseum, Bern, 1958, no. 82.
      Museum Boymans-van Beuningen, Rotterdam, 1958-59.
      Akademie der Bildenden Künste, Vienna, 1959, no. 60.

65

65. NUDE BY THE WICKER CHAIR. 1929.
    Oil on canvas, 48¼ x 39⅜″ (122,5 x 100 cm.).
    Not signed or dated.
    Collection Munch-museet, Oslo.
    Provenance: Gift of the artist.
    Exhibitions: Raadhushallen, Copenhagen, 1946, no. 85.
                 Liljevalchs Konsthall, Stockholm, 1947, no. 136.
                 Institute of Contemporary Art, Boston, 1950, no. 60.
                 Edvard Munch, Brighton, 1951-52, no. 59.
                 Gemeentemuseum, The Hague, 1952, no. 60.
                 Petit Palais, Paris, 1952, no. 58.

66

66. THE FIGHT. 1935.
   Oil on canvas, 41½ x 47⅜″ (105,5 x 120,5 cm.).
   Not signed or dated.
   Collection Munch-museet, Oslo.
   Provenance: Gift of the artist.
   Exhibitions: Harald Holst Halvorsen, Oslo, 1938, no. 3 b.
              Raadhushallen, Copenhagen, 1946, no. 90.
              Liljevalchs Konsthall, Stockholm, 1947, no. 142.
              Institute of Contemporary Art, Boston, 1950, no. 62.
              Edvard Munch, Brighton, 1951, no. 61.
              Gemeentemuseum, The Hague. 1951-52, no. 62.
              Petit Palais, Paris, 1952, no. 60.

67. "BETWEEN CLOCK AND BED" SELF-PORTRAIT. 1940-42.
Oil on canvas, 58¾ x 47½″ (149,5 x 120,5 cm.).
Not signed or dated.
Collection Munch-museet, Oslo.
Provenance: Gift of the artist.
Exhibitions: Raadhushallen, Copenhagen, 1946, no. 92.
Liljevalchs Konsthall, Stockholm, 1947, no. 144.
Institute of Contemporary Art, Boston, 1950, no. 63.
Edvard Munch, Brighton, 1951, no. 62.
Gemeentemuseum, The Hague, 1951-52, no. 63.
Petit Palais, Paris, 1952, no. 61.
Kunsthaus, Zürich, 1952, no. 77.
Palais des Beaux-Arts, Brussels, 1952, no. 23.
XXVII Biennale, Venice, 1954, no. 43.
Haus der Kunst, Munich, 1954, no. 103.
Palazzo delle Esposizione, Rome, 1955, no. 4081.

67

14 a.

14 a. MYSTIC SHORE. 1892.
    Oil on canvas, 33¾ x 49½″ (85.7 x 126.4 cm.).
    Signed l.l. "E. Munch 92".
    Collection Haakon Thomas Onstad, Munkedal, Sweden.

No. 14, MYSTIC SHORE, illustrated on page 38, is erroneously identi-
fied as the above painting owned by Haakon Thomas Onstad,
Munkedal. The version shown on page 38 belongs to the collection
of Gunnar Johnson Höst, Gothenburg, and is not included in the
exhibition.

Mr. Onstad's work is correctly recorded in J. P. Hodin's *Edvard
Munch*, Stockholm, Neuer Verlag, 1948, no. 95, but is incorrectly re-
produced as no. 10 in *Edvard Munch*, exhibition catalogue, Steinernes Haus, Frankfort am Main, 1962-63. The painting shown as
no. 10 in the Frankfort catalogue belongs to Dr. Höst and is illustrated in Ingrid Langaard's *Edvard Munch, Modningsår*, Oslo,
Gyldendal Norsk Forlag, 1960, no. 81, p. 159.

WORKS ON PAPER

BY LOUISE AVERILL SVENDSEN

That Edvard Munch is a graphic artist of great distinction and international fame is established. His prints increased his reputation during his lifetime; since his death, exhibitions of his graphic work have circulated widely throughout the world. It has not been the purpose of the subsequent selection, therefore, to recapitulate his enormous versatility in this field, but rather to concentrate upon ideas and themes that concerned him as an artist. Examples of works on paper have been selected that, with few exceptions, relate directly in subject to those rendered in oil. A representative number of Munch's drawings and watercolors from the rich stores of the Munch Museum in Oslo, presented to the American public for the first time, are also added to the familiar prints.

Munch probably did not consider his drawings and watercolors on the same level as his paintings and prints. He rarely exhibited them outside Norway and infrequently in Oslo. In his large 1927 retrospective at the National Gallery in Berlin, 223 paintings, but only 21 watercolors and drawings, were displayed. His legendary disregard for a canvas once he was finished with it applies equally to works on paper. Unfortunately the fragile nature of paper has been less able than canvas to withstand the dampness and complete lack of care. Exquisite pencil drawings have been watersoaked; watercolors and crayon drawings, strong and bold as their analogous oil versions, have had whole sections torn away.

The sheer quantity of sketches that he left, 4,400 in the Munch Museum Collection, is, of course, fortuitous. Where another artist might have destroyed them, Munch's living and working habits permitted him to cast them aside, thus ironically insuring their survival. The collection ranges from boyhood drawings, carefully executed academic nudes, sketchbook jottings, through countless preparatory studies for paintings. Many are brilliant but evidently abandoned studies whose reverse sides have been covered with random drawings. Almost every medium is used as are combinations of media and a variety of techniques. The virtuosity of his technique as well as his intensity and his vibrant feeling for form is evidenced throughout. Yet the range of subjects is not great. For the most part, the drawings are variations on themes already expressed or to be expressed in oil.

These variations in the smaller scale enrich our appreciation of the creative possibilities the artist confronts in the gradual realization of his ideas. One can see, as in a little drawing of 1899, Munch putting down in ink and crayon the essential composition for the large scale *Dance of Life*, 1899-1900, at the National Gallery in Oslo. The central couple dances gravely in the foreground, while other pairs whirl around them with abandon. The final composition retains this contrast of mood although, by the addition of a maiden and an older woman, a new and more complicated symbolism is introduced. In three studies for *The Death Bed*, 1895, in the Rasmus Meyer Collection in Bergen, the artist creates three different groupings of the mourners. In one, he brushes in broadly four figures at the head of the bed, one on one side and three opposite, who watch with agonized gestures the pale face on the pillow. In a charcoal study, the figure to the left is reduced to a bent head and an arm flung out across the counterpane; the group at the right is condensed into a bearded old man turned away from the tragic scene. In a small pencil sketch Munch achieves the arrangement that he eventually incorporates into the oil version. His viewpoint is now behind the bed so that all we can see is the back of the head on the pillow. The old man wrings his hands over the edge of the bed in the middle ground; a woman wails beside him. Other figures are indicated in the background, but the artist has reduced them to shadowy contours. These, in the final version, take their places beside the old man; the wailing woman now stands tight-lipped, controlled.

Finished studies unrelated to paintings are few—a harbor view, a self-portrait head in crayon, a pencil landscape, a watercolor of a model's head, a nude caught in the instant of undressing, to mention those chosen for this exhibition—but even these may reappear in the background of a land-scape or a life-size self-portrait. However closely a study may correspond to a given canvas or however independent it may appear, it remains a separate work in its effect. The unity of rapid movement between the starlit sky and the snow-covered pointed trees, in a charcoal version of *Starry Night*, 1923-24, has been replaced in the oil by slower rhythms of broad planes of snow and low masses of trees. The mood has shifted. For Munch the possibilities of ideas could never be exhausted. His sketches reflect his constant probing for deeper meanings, more sensitive nuances within the same theme.

Munch was a mature artist in his 30's when he was introduced to printmaking. His earliest experiments were in drypoint during the winter of 1894 in Berlin; later that year he produced his first lithograph and in 1896 he began working with woodcuts. During these very productive years, he used the graphic media primarily to recreate the subjects of his paintings, particularly those of the 80's and early 90's. In *The Sick Child*, 1894, he reproduces the impressionist painting of 1885-86 in drypoint. Here he has simplified the composition and has intensified the mood of grief and yearn-ing by sensitive contrasts of dark masses with delicate linear strokes.

The lithograph offered broader possibilities than the more intimate etching for working out directly and vividly problems relating to his paintings. Munch portrays the head of *The Sick Child*, 1896, in 4 colors in a series of lithographs which is one of his finest technical achievements. He utilizes the range of the medium to its fullest extent in adjusting and varying the colors to create tonal effects of the greatest subtlety.

It was in the medium of the woodcut, however, that Munch became not merely a master but a pioneer. Continuing along lines already indicated by Gauguin, he developed a technique which combined an emphasis on the quality of the woodblock surface, printing in flat tones and broad areas, and revealing the character of the stroke of the knife. He often sawed the block into sections which could then be inked and printed separately in a variety of colors. In *The Kiss*, 1898, Munch has used two blocks, first the silhouetted lovers and then over them a beautifully grained pine sur-face lightly inked. He has brought into harmony the inherent qualities of the wood and the expres-sive representation he sought in his paintings. In his woodcuts he achieved an originality of technique and style which profoundly influenced future generations of printmakers.

23

DRAWINGS AND WATERCOLORS

All of the works on paper have been lent from the Collection of Munch-museet, Oslo.

1. SIESTA. c. 1885. Pastel, 11½ x 14″ (29,1 x 35,8 cm.).

2. AT THE WINDOW. c. 1889. Crayon, 10⅝ x 9⅝″ (27 x 24,5 cm.).

3. FROM KARL JOHAN STREET, OSLO. c. 1892. Pencil and crayon, 13¼ x 9⅞″ (33,5 x 25,2 cm.).

4. ROSE AND AMÉLIE. 1893. Pencil, 14¼ x 15⅛″ (36,2 x 48,4 cm.).

5. AT THE DEATH BED. c. 1893. Gouache, 12⅜ x 13⅜″ (31,5 x 34,7 cm.).

6. AT THE DEATH BED. c. 1893. Pencil, 9 x 12½″ (23 x 31,7 cm.).

7. AT THE DEATH BED. c. 1893. Charcoal, 16⅝ x 19″ (42,2 x 48,1 cm.).

8. CONSOLATION. c. 1894. Charcoal, 14⅞ x 24¼″ (47,8 x 62,8 cm.).

9. MODEL STUDY. c. 1894. Charcoal and ink, 24¼ x 18½″ (61,5 x 47 cm.).

10. TWO WOMEN. c. 1895. Charcoal, 18⅛ x 14″ (47,2 x 35,5 cm.).

11. MYSTIC SHORE. 1895. Ink, 11¾ x 16″ (29,8 x 40,8 cm.).

12. ARTIST WITH A LYRE. c. 1896-97. Pencil and watercolor, 25 x 18⅞″ (63,5 x 48 cm.).

13. DANCE OF LIFE. c. 1899. Ink and crayon, 12¾ x 18¾″ (32,5 x 47,7 cm.).

14. SHORE AT ÅSGÅRDSTRAND. c. 1900. Pencil, 11¼ x 16½″ (28,7 x 42 cm.).

15. DRAWING FOR "GHOSTS". 1906. Charcoal, 10½ x 14½″ (26,7 x 37 cm.).

16. FEMALE NUDE AT THE WINDOW. c. 1907. Charcoal, watercolor and gouache, 24 x 19⅜″ (60,9 x 49,3 cm.).

17. FROM KRAGERØ. c. 1910. Watercolor, pencil and crayon, 18⅝ x 23⅞″ (47,2 x 60,7 cm.).

18. LANDSCAPE STUDY. c. 1912. Crayon, 8¼ x 10½″ (20,9 x 26,6 cm.).

19. WORKERS IN THE DRIVE. c. 1920. Charcoal, 18⅞ x 23½″ (48 x 59,8 cm.).

20. ON THE VERANDA. 1923. Crayon, 19¾ x 12¼″ (50,2 x 31,2 cm.).

21. STARRY NIGHT. c. 1923. Charcoal, 26⅜ x 24⅛″ (67 x 61,4 cm.).

22. MODEL UNDRESSING. c. 1925. Crayon and watercolor, 13⅞ x 10″ (35,3 x 25,3 cm.).

23. STUDY OF A HEAD, BIRGITTE. c. 1927-28. Watercolor, 13⅜ x 9¾″ (34,7 x 24,7 cm.). (Illustration page 97.)

24. SELF-PORTRAIT. c. 1930. Crayon, 15¾ x 10⅝″ (40 x 27 cm.).

ENGRAVINGS AND ETCHINGS

Sch. refers to the definitive catalogues of Munch's prints by Gustav Schiefler:
Verzeichnis des Graphischen Werks Edvard Munchs bis 1906, Berlin, Bruno Cassirer, 1907,
and *Edvard Munch. Das Graphische Werk 1906-1926*, Berlin, Euphorion, 1928.
W. refers to *Edvard Munch. Etchings* by Sigurd Willoch, Oslo, Johan Grundt Tanum, 1950.

25. THE SICK CHILD. 1894. Drypoint, 11⅝ x 10½″ (36 x 26,7 cm.). Sch. 7 V d; W. 7.

26. IN THE DIGS. 1895. Etching and drypoint, 8 x 12¼″ (20,3 x 31,2 cm.). Sch. 12 a III; W. 11.

27. THE KISS. 1895. Etching, aquatint, and drypoint, 13 x 10¼″ (33 x 26 cm.). Sch. 22 a; W. 22.

28. THE LONELY ONES. 1895. Etching, aquatint, drypoint, and roulette, 6⅛ x 8⅜″ (15,4 x 21,2 cm.). Sch. 20 V; W. 19.

29. MOONLIGHT. 1895. Drypoint and aquatint, 12¼ x 10⅛″ (31 x 25,5 cm.). Sch. 13 III; W. 12.

30. THE VOICE. 1895. Etching and aquatint, 9½ x 12¼″ (24 x 31 cm.). Sch. 19 b III; W. 18.

31. THE NURSE. 1908-09. Drypoint, 8¼ x 5⅞″ (20,5 x 15,2 cm.). Sch. 269 II; W. 140.

32. ADAM AND EVE. 1915. Etching with roulette and needle, 10¼ x 15″ (26 x 38 cm.). Sch. 430 b; W. 174.

33. GALLOPING HORSE. 1915. Etching, 15⅛ x 12⅝″ (38,5 x 32,2 cm.). Sch. 431; W. 175.

WOODCUTS

34. ANXIETY. 1896. 17⅞ x 14⅝″ (45,5 x 37,2 cm.). Sch. 62 b.

35. MOONLIGHT. 1896. 16⅛ x 18⅜″ (41 x 46,7 cm.). Sch. 81 A b.

36. THE KISS. 1897. 23 x 18″ (58,5 x 45,7 cm.). Sch. 102 A.

37. THE KISS. 1898. 16¼ x 18⅜″ (41,2 x 46,2 cm.). Sch. 102 C.

38. FERTILITY. 1898. 16½ x 20⅜″ (41,9 x 51,8 cm.). Sch. 110.

39. THE LONELY ONES. 1899. 15½ x 21½″ (39,5 x 53,0 cm.). Sch. 133.

40. MYSTIC SHORE. 1899. 14½ x 22½″ (37,2 x 57,2 cm.). Sch. 125 a.

41. BIRGITTE III. 1930. 23¼ x 12⅝″ (59,6 x 32,2 cm.).

LITHOGRAPHS

42. THE CRY. 1895. 14 x 10″ (35,4 x 25,4 cm.). Sch. 32.

43. MADONNA. 1895. 24 x 17⅜″ (61 x 44,1 cm.). Sch. 33 A II a.

44. SELF-PORTRAIT WITH SKELETON ARM. 1895. 18 x 12½″ (45,6 x 31,6 cm.). Sch. 31.

45. VAMPIRE. 1895. 15⅛ x 21⅞″ (38,5 x 55,5 cm.). Sch. 34 b.

46. DEATH BED. 1896. 15¾ x 19⅝″ (40 x 49,8 cm.). Sch. 72.

47. THE SICK CHILD. 1896. 16⅝ x 22¼″ (42,1 x 56,5 cm.). Sch. 59 c.

48. THE SICK CHILD. 1896. 16⅝ x 22¼″ (42,1 x 56,5 cm.). Sch. 59 c.

49. THE SICK CHILD. 1896. 16½ x 22½″ (42 x 57 cm.). Sch. 59 d.

50. NUDE WITH RED HAIR (SIN). 1901. 27⅜ x 15½″ (69,6 x 39,5 cm.). Sch. 142 c.

51. JEALOUSY. 1902. 18½ x 22½″ (47 x 57,2 cm.). Sch. 58.

52. MADONNA. 1902. 24 x 17⅜″ (61 x 44,1 cm.). Sch. 33 A II b 1.

53. MADONNA WITH THE BROOCH (EVA MUDOCCI). 1903. 25¾ x 18½″ (64,8 x 46,8 cm.). Sch. 212.

54. PROFESSOR K. E. SCHREINER. 1930. 24 x 19⅞″ (60,8 x 50,5 cm.).

DOCUMENTATION

In general only exhibitions which refer to specific paintings in this exhibition are listed in the following documentation section. A few major exhibitions have been added.

ONE MAN EXHIBITIONS

STUDENTS' ASSOCIATION, Oslo, April 20-May 12, 1889.

JEWELER TOSTRUP'S BUILDING, Oslo, September 14-October 4, 1892. *Edvard Munchs Maleriudstilling.*

ARCHITEKTENHAUS (Verein Berliner Künstler), Berlin, November 5-12, 1892.

EDUARD SCHULTE, Düsseldorf, November 1892; EDUARD SCHULTE, Cologne, November-December 1892. *Sonder-Ausstellung des Malers Edvard Munch aus Christiana vom November 5-19.*

EQUITABLE-PALAST, Berlin, December 26, 1892-January 1893.

GEORG KLEIS, Copenhagen, February 24-March 14, 1893. *Den Norske Maler, Eduard Munchs samlede Arbejder.*

THEODOR LICHTENBERG NACHFOLGER FERDINAND MORAWE, Victoria-haus, Dresden, May 1893. *Sonder-Ausstellung von Werken des Malers Eduard Munch.*

UGO BARROCCIO, Berlin, December 1893. *Eduard Munch Gemälde-Ausstellung.*

GALERIE BLANCHE, Stockholm, October 1-31, 1894. *Förteckning öfver Edvard Munch Utställningen.*

UGO BARROCCIO, Berlin, March 3-24, 1895. *Sonder-Ausstellung des Edv. Munch.*

BLOMQVISTS LOKALE, Oslo, October 1895; Bergen, November 1895; Stavanger, Norway, January 1896.

S. BING, Paris, June 1896. *Salon de l'Art Nouveau.*

DIORAMALOKALET, Oslo, September 15-October 17, 1897.

DIORAMALOKALET, Oslo, 1900. *Edvard Munch. Maleriudstilling i Dioramalokalet.* Catalogue introduction by Munch quoting criticism by Edouard Gérard, Paris.

ARNO WOLFFRAMM (DRESDENER KUNSTSALON), Dresden, 1900. *Sonder-Ausstellung von Edvard Munch.*

HOLLAENDERGAARDEN, Oslo, October 1901. *Edvard Munchs Udstilling.*

BLOMQVISTS LOKALE, Oslo, September 16, 1903. *Edvard Munchs Udstilling Blomqvists Lokale.* Catalogue introductions by Hans Rosenhagen, Gustav Schiefler and Marius-Ary Leblond.

DIORAMALOKALET, Oslo, October-November 15, 1904. *Edvard Munchs Udstilling.*

GALERIE "MANES", Prague, February 5-March 12, 1905. Catalogue introduction by K. Svoboda.

GROSSHERZOGLICHES MUSEUM, Weimar, from November 11, 1906.

OTTO FISCHER, Bielefeld, Germany, April 6-30, 1907.

ATENEUMIN TAIDEMUSEO, Helsinki, January 3-31, 1909.

BLOMQVISTS LOKALE, Oslo, March 1909; BERGENS KUNSTFORENING, Bergen, Summer 1909.

DIORAMALOKALET, Oslo, March 1910. *Edvard Munchs Udstilling i Dioramalokalet.*

DIORAMALOKALET, Oslo, April 1911. *Edvard Munch-Udstilling i Dioramalokalet.*

MODERNE GALERIE THANNHAUSER, Munich, February 1912, *Kollektiv-Ausstellung Edvard Munch.*

SONDERBUND WESTDEUTSCHER KUNSTFREUNDE UND KÜNSTLER, Cologne, May 25-September 30, 1912.

SALONG JOËL, Stockholm, February 1913. *Målningar och Grafisk Konst af Edvard Munch.*

KONSTNÄRSHUSET, Stockholm, September 1913. *Edvard Munch.*

GALERIE FRITZ GURLITT, Berlin, February 1914. *Edvard Munch.*

BLOMQVISTS LOKALE, Oslo, October 1918. *Edvard Munch 1918.* Catalogue introduction by Edvard Munch.

KUNSTHAUS, Zürich, June 18-August 2, 1922. *Ausstellung Edvard Munch in Züricher Kunsthaus.* Catalogue introduction by W. Wartmann.

STÄDTISCHE KUNSTHALLE, Mannheim, November 7, 1926-January 9, 1927. *Edvard Munch. Gemälde und Graphik.* Catalogue introduction by G. F. Hartlaub.

NATIONALGALERIE, Berlin, March 15-May 15, 1927. *Edvard Munch.* Catalogue introduction by Ludwig Justi.

NASJONALGALLERIET, Oslo, 1927. *Edvard Munch.* Catalogue introductions by Jens Thiis and Ludwig Justi.

KUNSTHÜTTE, Chemnitz, Germany, November 15-December 11, 1929. *Ausstellung Edvard Munch.* Catalogue introduction by Will Grohmann.

DRESDEN, June-September 1929. *Künstler-Vereinigung.*

THE LONDON GALLERY, London, October 20-November 14, 1936. *Edvard Munch.* Catalogue introduction by Herbert Read.

KUNGLIGA AKADEMIEN FÖR DE FRIA KONSTERNA, Stockholm, March 1937. *Sveriges Allmänna Konstförening Edvard Munch utställning.* Catalogue introductions by Pola Gauguin and Sigge Bergstrom.

STEDELIJK MUSEUM, Amsterdam, May 1-June 20, 1937. *Edvard Munch.* Catalogue introduction by Pola Gauguin.

HARALD HOLST HALVORSENS KUNSTHANDEL, Oslo, September 1938. *Utstilling av Edvard Munch.*

NATIONALMUSEUM, Stockohlm; and KONSTMUSEUM, Gothenburg, Sweden, February 1944. *Edvard Munch. Oljemålningar, grafik, och teckningar i svensk och norsk ägo i Sverige.* Catalogue introductions by Erik Wettergren, Axel L. Romdahl, Folke Holmér and Gunnar Jungmarker.

RAADHUSHALLEN, Copenhagen, April 8-25, 1946. *Mindeudstillingen for Edvard Munch i Københavns Raadhus.* Catalogue introduction by Johan H. Langaard.

LILJEVALCHS KONSTHALL, Stockholm, January 4-February 2, 1947; GÖTEBORGS KONSTMUSEUM, Gothenburg, February 25-March 16, 1947. *Edvard Munch.* Catalogue introduction by Johan H. Langaard.

INSTITUTE OF CONTEMPORARY ART, Boston, April 19-May 19, 1950; PHILLIPS GALLERY, Washington, D.C., May 28-June 20, 1950; THE MUSEUM OF MODERN ART, New York, June 30-August 13, 1950; DETROIT INSTITUTE OF ARTS, September 1-29, 1950; MINNEAPOLIS INSTITUTE OF FINE ARTS, October 12-November 9, 1950; COLORADO SPRINGS FINE ARTS CENTER, November 23-December 21, 1950; LOS ANGELES COUNTY MUSEUM, January 4-February 1, 1951; M. H. DE YOUNG MEMORIAL MUSEUM, San Francisco, February 10-March 10, 1951; CARNEGIE INSTITUTE, Pittsburgh, March 24-April 21, 1951; THE ART INSTITUTE OF CHICAGO, May 7-June 10, 1951; CITY ART MUSEUM OF ST. LOUIS, June 18-July 15, 1951. *Edvard Munch.* Catalogue introductions by Frederick B. Deknatel and Johan H. Langaard.

Cologne, Hamburg, Lübeck, Summer 1951. *Austellung Edvard Munch 1863-1944.* Catalogue introduction by L. Reidemeister.

THE ARTS COUNCIL OF GREAT BRITAIN, *Edvard Munch, An Exhibition of Paintings, Etchings, and Lithographs*, Brighton, September 1-22, 1951; Glasgow, October 1-22, 1951; TATE GALLERY, London, October 31-December 2, 1951. Catalogue introductions by Philip James and Johan H. Langaard. Substantially the same as the American traveling exhibition, 1950-51.

KUNSTNERNES HUS, Oslo, November 10-December 16, 1951. *Edvard Munch. Utstilling malerier, akvareller, tegninger, grafikk.*

GEMEENTEMUSEUM, The Hague, December 13, 1951-February 15, 1952. *Edvard Munch.* Catalogue introduction by Johan H. Langaard. Continuation of The Arts Council of Great Britain exhibition.

PETIT PALAIS, Paris, March-April 1952. *E. Munch.* Catalogue introductions by Paul Coirre, André Chamson and Johan H. Langaard.

KUNSTHAUS, Zürich, June 22-August 17, 1952. *Munch.* Catalogue introductions by R. Wehrli and W. Wartmann.

PALAIS DES BEAUX-ARTS, Brussels, October 11-November 2, 1952. *Edvard Munch.* Catalogue introduction by Johan H. Langaard.

XXVII BIENNALE, Venice, 1954. *Esposizione Biennale Internazionale d'Arte.* Catalogue introduction by Leif Østby.

HAUS DER KUNST, Munich, November-December 1954; Cologne, 1955. *Edvard Munch.* Catalogue introductions by Sigurd Willoch and Ernst Buchner.

KUNSTFORENINGEN, Copenhagen, March 5-27, 1955; FYNS STIFTSMU-SEUM, Odense, Denmark, April 1955. *Edvard Munch Udstilling.* Catalogue introductions by F. L. Crone, Sigurd Willoch, Pola Gauguin.

KUNSTNERFORBUNDET, Oslo, January 25-February 20, 1958. *Munch-bilder i privat eie.*

KUNSTMUSEUM, Bern, October 7-November 30, 1958. *Edvard Munch.* Catalogue introduction by Max Huggler.

MUSEUM BOYMANS-VAN BEUNINGEN, Rotterdam, December 10, 1958-February 8, 1959. *Edvard Munch.*

MUSEUM VOOR STADT EN LANDE, Groningen, The Netherlands, February 20-March 16, 1959. *Edvard Munch.*

AKADEMIE DER BILDENDEN KÜNSTE, Vienna, May 22-July 5, 1959. *Edvard Munch.* Catalogue introductions by Hofrat Hans Mandl and Fritz Novotny.

MUSEUM NARODOWE, Warsaw, November 2-December 15, 1959. *Edvard Munch, Malarstwo Grafika.* Catalogue introductions by Johan H. Langaard and Professor Dr. Julius Starzynski.

STEINERNES HAUS, Frankfurt am Main, November 9, 1962-January 6, 1963. Catalogue introduction by Ewald Rathke.

RUHRFESTSPIELE, Recklinghausen, 1965.

GROUP EXHIBITIONS

RIKSHOSPITALETS LOKALER, Oslo, 1884. *Annual State Exhibition.*

Second Annual State Exhibition, Oslo, 1885.

Annual State Exhibition, Oslo, 1886.

Annual State Exhibition, Oslo, 1888.

Annual State Exhibition, Oslo, 1890.

PALAIS DES ARTS LIBEREAUX, Paris, April 1-May 31, 1896. *12 Salon des Indépendants.*

SECESSION, Berlin, 1902. *Fünften Kunstausstellung der Berliner Secession.*

SECESSION, Vienna, December 1903-February 1904.

SECESSION, Berlin, 1908.

ATENEUMIN TAIDEMUSEO, Helsinki, February- March 1911.

KÜNSTLERBUND HAGEN, Vienna, January-February 1912, *Norwegische Künstler.*

THE AMERICAN ART GALLERIES, New York, December 10-25, 1912. Traveled 1912-13 to Buffalo, Toledo, Chicago, Boston. *Exhibition of Contemporary Scandinavian Art.* Held under the auspices of the American-Scandinavian Society. Catalogue introductions by Christian Brinton, Karl Madsen, Jens Thiis and Carl G. Laurin.

GALERIE ALFRED FLECHTHEIM, Düsseldorf, March 28-April 17, 1914. *Edvard Munch, Ernst Barlach.*

DEN FRIE UDSTILLINGS BYGNING, Copenhagen, November 1915. *Kunstnernes Efteraars Udstilling.*

Copenhagen, November-December 1915. *Den Norske Kunstudstilling ved Charlottenborg.*

PALACE OF FINE ARTS, San Francisco, February 20-December 4, 1915. *Panama-Pacific International Exposition.*

LILJEVALCHS KONSTHALL, Stockholm, March-April 1917. *Nutida Norsk Konst.*

KONSTHALLEN, Gothenburg, 1923. *Jubileumsutställningen i Göteborg 1923. Nordisk Konst.* Catalogue introductions by Axel L. Romdahl and Jens Thiis.

Dresden, 1926. *International Exhibition.*

ROYAL SOCIETY, London, September 25-October 21, 1928. *Norwegian Exhibition.*

KUNSTHAUS, Zürich, February 20-March 20, 1932. *Edvard Munch, Paul Gauguin.*

KUNSTNERNES HUS, Oslo, September 5-October 2, 1932. *Høstutstil-lingen gjennem de første 25 år 1882-1907.*

KUNGLIGA AKADEMIEN FÖR DE FRIA KONSTERNA, Stockholm, June 18-August 31, 1941. *Dansk, Finsk, Isländsk och Norsk Konst ur samlingar i Sverige.*

M. H. DE YOUNG MEMORIAL MUSEUM, San Francisco, 1945. *United Nations-Norway.*

ALLEN MEMORIAL ART MUSEUM, Oberlin College, Oberlin, Ohio, 1946. *Five Expressionists.*

KUNSTNERNES HUS, Oslo, January 10-25, 1948. *Rolf Stenersens sam-ling.* Catalogue introduction by Reidar Revold.

GEMEENTEMUSEUM, The Hague, December 17, 1949-February 4, 1950. *Honderd Jaar Noorse Schilderkunst.*

PALAIS DES BEAUX-ARTS, Brussels, March 4-26, 1950. *Un Siècle de Peinture Norvegienne.*

UNIVERSITY OF MINNESOTA ART GALLERY, Minneapolis, 1952. *Space in Painting.*

PALAZZO DELLE ESPOSIZIONI, Rome, April-May, 1955. *Finlandia, Dani-marca, Islanda, Norvegia, Svezia, Arte Nordica Contemporanea.* Catalogue introduction by Reidar Revold.

NATIONALMUSEUM, Stockholm, April-June, 1956; KUNSTHAUS, Zürich, 1957; GEMEENTEMUSEUM, The Hague, April 19-June 11, 1957. *Ragnar Moltzau Collection.*

KUNSTNERFORBUNDET, Oslo, February 9-21, 1957. *Naeringslivet i Kunsten.*

STEDELIJK MUSEUM, Amsterdam, July 6-September 30, 1957. *Europa 1907.*

PALAIS INTERNATIONAL DES BEAUX-ARTS, Brussels, April 17- July 21, 1958. *Exposition Universelle et Internationale de Bruxelles. 50 Ans d'Art Moderne.* Catalogue introduction by Em. Langui.

PALAIS DES EXPOSITION, Charleroi, Belgium, July 5-September 14, 1958. *Art et Travail.*

THE MUSEUM OF MODERN ART, New York, June 6-September 6, 1960; CARNEGIE INSTITUTE, Pittsburgh, October 13-December 12, 1960; LOS ANGELES COUNTY MUSEUM, January 17-March 5, 1961; THE BALTIMORE MUSEUM OF ART, April 1-May 15, 1961. *Art Nouveau.* Catalogue introductions by Peter Selz, Greta Daniel, Henry-Russel Hitchcock, Alan M. Fern.

MUSÉE NATIONAL D'ART MODERNE, Paris, November 4, 1960-January 23, 1961. *Les Sources du XXe Siècle, Les Arts en Europe de 1884 à 1914.* Catalogue introductions by Jean Cassou, Guilio Carlo Argan, Nicolaus Pevsner.

KUNSTNERFORBUNDET, Oslo, January 14-25, 1961. *Kunstnerforbundet 50 År. Utstilling I.*

Darmstadt, 1963. *Zeugnisse der Angst.*

LOUISIANA MUSEUM, Copenhagen, October 16-November 1963. *Rolf Stenersens Samling.*

MARLBOROUGH-GERSON GALLERY, New York, November - December 1963. *Artist and Maecenas. A Tribute to Curt Valentin.*

HAUS DER KUNST, Munich, March 14-May 10, 1964. *Secession Euro-päische Kunst um die Jahrhundertwende.* Catalogue introduc-tion by Siegfried Wichmann.

NASJONALGALLERIET, Oslo, May 5-June 7, 1964. *Jubileumsutstilling 1814-1964.*

KUNSTHALLE, Kiel, Germany, June 24-July 26, 1964, *150 Jahre Nor-wegische Malerei.* Catalogue introductions by Sigurd Willoch, Hans Tintelnot and Leif Østby.

PALAIS DE BEAULIEU, Lausanne, 1964. *Chefs-d'Oeuvre des Collections Suisses de Manet à Picasso.* Catalogue introduction by Max Huggler.

THE SOLOMON R. GUGGENHEIM MUSEUM, New York, May-September 1964. *Van Gogh and Expressionism.* Catalogue introduction by Maurice Tuchman.

SELECTED BIBLIOGRAPHY

PRZYBYSZEWSKI, STANISLAW, ed. *Das Werk des Edvard Munch. Berlin,* S. Fischer Verlag, 1894. Contributions by Stanislaw Przybyszewski, Franz Servaes, Willy Pastor, Julius Meier-Graefe.

LINDE, MAX. *Edvard Munch und die Kunst der Zukunft.* Berlin, F. Gottenheimer, 1905. Earlier edition 1902.

ESSWEIN, HERMANN. *Edvard Munch.* Munich and Leipzig, R. Piper and Co., 1905.

SCHIEFLER, GUSTAV. *Verzeichnis des graphischen Werkes Edvard Munchs bis 1906.* Berlin, Bruno Cassirer, 1907.

GLASER, CURT. *Edvard Munch* Berlin, Bruno Cassirer, 1917.

SCHIEFLER, GUSTAV. *Edvard Munch. Das graphische Werk 1906-1926.* Berlin, Euphorion Verlag, 1928.

LANGAARD, JOHAN H. *Edvard Munch. Maleren.* Oslo, Nasjonalgalleriet Veileder IV, 1932.

GAUGUIN, POLA. *Edvard Munch.* Oslo, Gyldendal, 1932. New edition 1946.

THIIS, JENS. *Edvard Munch og hans samtid.* Oslo, Gyldendal, 1933. German edition translated by Joachim Dieter Bloch, Berlin, Rembrandt Verlag, 1934.

GAUGUIN, POLA. *Grafikeren Edvard Munch. Litografier.* Trondheim, Brun, 1946.

GAUGUIN, POLA. *Grafikeren Edvard Munch. Tresnitt og raderinger.* Trondheim, Brun, 1946.

STENERSEN, ROLF E. *Edvard Munch. Naerbilled av et geni.* Stockholm, 1944, Copenhagen, 1945, Oslo, 1945. Enlarged edition, Oslo, Gyldendal, 1946.

Edvard Munch, som vi kjente ham. Oslo, Dreyers Forlag, 1946. Contributions by K. E. Schreiner, Christian Gierløff, Pola Gauguin, Johs. Roede, Ingeborg Motzfeld Löchen, Titus Vile Müller, Birgit Prestøe, David Bergendahl, L. O. Ravensberg.

Edvard Munchs Selvportretter. Oslo, Gyldendal Norsk Forlag, 1947. Introduction by Johan H. Langaard.

Edvard Munch, Memnesket og Kunstneren. Oslo, Gyldendal Norsk Forlag, Kunst og Kultur Series, 1946. Contributions by Christian Gierløff, Axel L. Romdahl, Pola Gauguin, Johan H. Langaard, Karl Stenerud, N. Rygg, Erik Pedersen, Birgit Prestøe, Chrix Dahl.

SARVIG, OLE. *Edvard Munchs Grafik.* Copenhagen, J. H. Schultz Forlag, 1948. New edition, Copenhagen, Gyldendal, 1964. German edition, Zürich-Stuttgart, Flamberg, 1964.

HODIN, J. P. *Edvard Munch. Der Genius des Nordens.* Stockholm, Neuer Verlag, 1948. New edition, Mainz, Florian Kupferberg Verlag, 1963.

Edvard Munchs brev. Familien. Oslo, Johan Grundt Tanums Forlag, 1949.

DEKNATEL, FREDERICK B. *Edvard Munch.* New York, Chanticleer Press, 1950.

WILLOCH, SIGURD. *Edvard Munchs Raderinger.* Oslo, Johan Grundt Tanum, 1950.

STENERSEN, ROLF E. *Edvard Munch.* Zürich, Büchergilde Gutenberg, 1949. Later edition, Stockholm, Neuer Verlag, 1950.

GIERLØFF, CHRISTIAN. *Edvard Munch selv.* Oslo, Gyldendal, 1953.

KOKOSCHKA, OSKAR. *Der Expressimus Edvard Munchs.* Vienna, Gurlitt, 1953.

SVENAEUS, GÖSTA. *Ide och innehäll i Edvard Munchs konst. En analys av Aulamålningarna.* Oslo, Gyldendal, 1953.

Edvard Munchs brev fra Dr. Max Linde. Oslo, Dreyers Forlag, 1954.

GERLACH, HANS EGON. *Edvard Munch. Sein Leben und sein Werk.* Hamburg, Christian Wegner, 1955.

GLØERSEN, INGER ALVER. *Den Munch jeg møtte.* Oslo, Gyldendal, 1956.

LANGAARD, JOHAN H. AND REVOLD, REIDAR. *Edvard Munch som tegner.* Oslo, Kunsten Idag, 1958. English edition, *The Drawings of Edvard Munch.* Oslo, Kunsten Idag, 1958.

MOEN, ARVE. *Samtid og miljø.* Oslo, Forlaget Norsk Kunstreproduksjon, 1956. English edition, *Age and Milieu.* Oslo, Forlaget Norsk Kunstreproduksjon, 1956. German edition, *Edvard Munch. Sein Zeit und sein Milieu. Ein Bildwerk.* Munich, F. Bruckmann, 1959.

MOEN, ARVE. *Edvard Munch. Kvinnen og eros.* Oslo, Forlaget Norsk Kunstreproduksjon, 1957. English edition, *Woman and Eros.* Oslo, Forlaget Norsk Kunstreproduksjon, 1957. German edition, *Edvard Munch. Der Künstler und die Frauen. Ein Bildwerk.* Munich, F. Bruckmann, 1959.

MOEN, ARVE. *Edvard Munch. Landskap og dyr. Et Billedverk.* Oslo, Forlaget Norsk Kunstreproduksjon, 1958. English edition, *Nature and Animals.* Oslo, Forlaget Norsk Kunstreproduksjon, 1958. German edition, *Edvard Munch. Tier und Landschaft. Ein Bildwerk.* Munich, F. Bruckmann, 1959.

BENESCH, OTTO. *Edvard Munch.* London, The Phaidon Press, 1960. German edition, *Edvard Munch.* Cologne, Phaidon Verlag, 1960.

LANGAARD, JOHAN H. AND REVOLD, REIDAR. Edvard Munch. *Auladekorasjonene.* Oslo, Forlaget Norsk Kunstreproduksjon, 1960. English edition *Edvard Munch. The University Murals.* Oslo, Forlaget Norsk Kunstreproduksjon, 1960.

LANGAARD, INGRID, *Edvard Munch. Modningsår.* Oslo, Gyldendal, 1960.

MOHR, OTTO LOUS. *Edvard Munchs Auladekorasjoner.* Oslo, Gyldendal, 1960.

Oslo Kommunes Kunstsamlinger, Årböker. Oslo, 1951, 1960, 1963. Detailed bibliographies by Hannah B. Müller and Reidar Revold.

LANGAARD, JOHAN H. AND REVOLD, REIDAR. *Edvard Munch fra år til år. A Year by Year Record of Edvard Munch's Life.* Oslo, H. Aschehoug and Co., 1961.

LANGAARD, JOHAN H. AND REVOLD, REIDAR. *Mesterverker i Munchmuseet Oslo.* Oslo, Forlaget Norsk Kunstreproduksjon, 1963. German edition, *Meisterwerke in Munch-Museum, Oslo.* Stuttgart, An. Belser Verlag, 1963. English edition, *Edvard Munch.* New York, Toronto, McGraw-Hill, and Co., 1964.

GREVE, ELI. *Edvard Munch. Liv og verk i lys av tresnittene.* Oslo, J. W. Cappelens Forlag, 1963.

THE SOLOMON R. GUGGENHEIM MUSEUM

STAFF

Director	*Thomas M. Messer*
Curator	*Lawrence Alloway*
Associate Curator	*Louise Averill Svendsen*
Research Fellows	*Carol Fuerstein and Rose Carol Washton*
Librarian	*Mary Joan Hall*
Public Affairs	*Everett Ellin*
Membership	*Carol Tormey*
Registrar	*Alice Hildreth Goldman*
Conservation	*Orrin Riley and Saul Fuerstein*
Photography	*Robert E. Mates*
Custodian	*Jean Xceron*
Business Administrator	*Glenn H. Easton, Jr.*
Administrative Assistant	*Viola H. Gleason*
Office Manager	*Agnes R. Connolly*
Purchasing Agent	*Elizabeth M. Funghini*
Sales Supervisor	*Joseph D. Griffin, Jr.*
Building Superintendent	*Peter G. Loggin*
Head Guard	*Fred C. Mahnken*

PHOTOGRAPHIC CREDITS   All photographs but the following were made by O. Vaering, Oslo:

The Detroit Institute of Arts, no. 53

Vladimir Fyman, Prague, no. 39

Marlborough-Gerson Gallery, Inc. New York, no. 38

The following color plates were lent by: Arts Magazine, New York, no. 28

Museum of Fine Arts, Boston, no. 19

Kunsthalle, Kiel, no. 18

Munch-museet, Oslo, nos. 49, 54, 67

Nationalgalleriet, Oslo, no. 1

Phaidon Press, London, nos. 9, 27, 30, 52, 58

Skira, Geneva, no. 6

Steinernes Haus, Frankfurt am Main, nos. 13, 21, 32, 48

Exhibition 65/6　　　　　　*October 1965-January 1966*

3,000 copies of this catalogue,
designed by Herbert Matter,
have been printed by Sterlip Press
in September 1965
for the Trustees of The Solomon R. Guggenheim Foundation
on the occasion of the exhibition
"Edvard Munch"